CO 1 58 813

GW01336473

SGA

C

SEAHAM
7/04
DC
Durham Clayport Library

5881337

DURHAM COUNTY COUNCIL
Arts, Libraries and Museums Department

Please return or renew this item by the last date shown.
Fines will be charged if the book is kept after this date.
Thank you for using *your* library.

100% recycled paper.

IS A MAST A MUST?

IS A MAST A MUST?

How to fight off intruders

Barry Bracewell-Milnes

The Book Guild Ltd
Sussex, England

First published in Great Britain in 2001 by
The Book Guild Ltd
25 High Street,
Lewes, East Sussex
BN7 2LU

Copyright © Barry Bracewell-Milnes 2001

The right of Barry Bracewell-Milnes to be identified as the author of this work has been asserted by him in accordance with the Copyright, Designs and Patents Act 1988.

All rights reserved. No part of this publication may be reproduced, transmitted, or stored in a retrieval system, in any form or by any means, without permission in writing from the publisher, nor be otherwise circulated in any form of binding or cover other than that in which it is published and without a similar condition being imposed on the subsequent purchaser.

Typesetting in Times by
Keyboard Services, Luton, Bedfordshire

Printed in Great Britain by
Bookcraft (Bath) Ltd, Avon

A catalogue record for this book is
available from the British Library

ISBN 1 85776 587 7

CONTENTS

Preface	ix
The author	x
The team	xii
The dramatis personae	xiii
Summary	xvi
1 Introduction	1
2 The problem	3
3 The Council	5
The obstacles	5
The Councillors	6
The application	7
The canvass	8
Correspondence with Caseley and Cowle	10
The Planning Committee	10
Waverley Council	12
The local press	12
The officials	13
4 The Residents' Association	15
5 The politicians : Buckpassers United	19
The Rt. Hon. Sir Archibald Hamilton, MP	19
Cabinet Ministers	21
The Rt. Hon. William Hague, MP	22

6	The businessmen	25
	The campaign	26
	The outcome	34
7	Other sites	36
	Nork Park	36
	Ruxley Lane, Ewell	39
	BBM Banstead Station	40
	Correspondence with BT and BT Cellnet	43
	A new vision for business	46
	Institutional incompetence?	48
	A tale of two companies	49
	Ten points for the operators	50
	The operators and the politicians	51
	No masts for Nork	51
8	How to fight back	53
	Legal and planning activities	54
	Environmental bodies	55
	Campaigning	56
9	Changing the law	61
	Council for the Protection of Rural England	62
	Other proposals	63
10	Outrage!	69

APPENDICES

A	The legislative background	71
B	John Popham and the Council	74
C	Circular of 20 March 1999 to local residents	78
D	Letter of 25 March 1999 to Brian Cowle	80

E	Letter of 23 March 1999 to Sir Archibald Hamilton	82
F	Letter of 24 March 1999 to the Prime Minister	85
G	Letter of 25 March 1999 to the Prime Minister	87
H	Letter of 26 March 1999 to the Prime Minister	89
I	Letter of 27 March 1999 to the Prime Minister	91
J	Letter of 20 March 1999 to John Fooks, Chairman of Sutton and East Surrey Water PLC (SESW)	94
K	Letter of 20 March 1999 to Lord MacLaurin of Knebworth, Chairman of Vodafone PLC	96
L	Circular of 28 March 1999 to residents of Nork Way, Warren Road and Fir Tree Road	99
M	Letter of 28 March 1999 to Phil Holder, Managing Director, SESW	101
N	Letter of 29 March 1999 to Phil Holder, Managing Director, SESW	103
O	Letter of 30 March 1999 to John Fooks, Chairman, SESW	106
P	Letter of 7 April 1999 to Lord MacLaurin of Knebworth, Chairman of Vodafone PLC	108
Q	Circular of 7 May 1999 from Mary Saunders	110
R	Ruxley Lane: Contribution from Councillor Mrs Jean Smith	112
S	Letter of 2 June 1999 to R. N. Clifford, Director of Environmental Services, Reigate and Banstead Borough Council	115
T	Letter of 1 May 1999 to Banstead Builders' Merchants (BBM)	119
U	Letter of 14 June 1999 to Nicholas Eldred, Company Secretary, BT Cellnet	121

V	Letter of 9 January 2000 to Sir Iain Vallance, Chairman, BT	124
W	The missing phone book	126
X	Council for the Protection of Rural England: Ten campaign tips	129

PREFACE

Telecommunication masts are breeding like rabbits. Nobody wants one in his backyard; but it is widely believed that resistance is futile. This is not so.

This book tells the story of a successful campaign in Spring 1999 against the erection of a mast in Nork, Banstead, Surrey. It discusses pressures brought to bear on the local Council and national politicians (which were ineffective) and on businessmen (which were effective). In order to succeed, a campaign like this has to operate in both these dimensions.

The story illustrates the defects in the present law on the subject, and the book ends with proposals for changes to reduce the present bias in favour of telecommunication operators and against the ordinary householder and citizen.

THE AUTHOR

Barry Bracewell-Milnes was sacked in 1973 by Mr Campbell Adamson, Director General of the Confederation of British Industry (CBI), for supporting capitalism, free enterprise and the market economy.

On the traditionalist side, he believes in the monarchy and the hereditary peerage. He was a member of the Oxford University Heraldry Society, although his heraldry is now rusty. He is a member of the Rutland Local History and Record Society and of Forward in Faith, the Prayer Book Society, the Society of King Charles the Martyr, the Royal Martyr Church Union and the Movement Against Bats in Churches.

On the capitalist side, he is a member of the British Property Federation and the Institute of Directors.

On the libertarian side, he is a member of the Adam Smith Institute, the Institute of Economic Affairs, the Libertarian Alliance, the Mont Pelerin Society, the Society for Individual Freedom and Survival (also known as Survival International and Survival for Tribal Peoples). He is a member of the Advisory Council of FOREST (Freedom Organisation for the Right to Enjoy Smoking Tobacco).

On the professional side, his memberships include the Association of Learned and Professional Society Publishers.

His first book *The Measurement of Fiscal Policy* was published by the CBI in 1971. (Now obtainable from the author at 26 Lancaster Court, Banstead, Surrey SM7 1RR.) His book

Tax Avoidance and Evasion: The Individual and Society (Panopticum Press, 1979; second impression, 1980) is currently being published in Swedish. He is at present working on *White Alchemy: the Costless Creation of Wealth in Economics, Religion and the Arts*. The present book is his twenty-fifth.

THE TEAM

Five of us contributed to the fight against the mast, myself and four others.

Dr Mary Saunders (Mary), a retired medical physicist, first alerted me to the danger of the mast and masterminded the legal and planning dimensions of our campaign. She secured the professional support of her brother.

John Popham (John), Mary's brother, an environmental and planning consultant specialising in cases of this kind, drafted the technical submissions to Reigate and Banstead Council.

Costa Sarafoglou (Costa), proprietor of Bespoke Designs (45 Nork Way, Banstead), did the artwork and faxing. It was Costa who suggested the title of the book, *Is a Mast a Must?*

My wife Ann did urgent typing, joined in the legwork, provided sound advice and moral support and helped to keep me sane.

THE DRAMATIS PERSONAE

Bachen, Dr Rolf — Resident of Ruxley Lane, Ewell
Bagwell, Nadia — Customer Resolution Executive, BT Cellnet
Caseley, M. K. — Case officer, Environmental Services Department, Reigate and Banstead Borough Council
Channing Williams, David — Managing Director of Vodafone
Clifford, Nigel — Director of Environmental Services, Reigate and Banstead Borough Council
Coates, Lee — Ethical Investors Group
Cowle, Brian — Mayor Elect/Mayor of Reigate and Banstead Borough Council
Crawley, Mrs J. — The Prime Minister's correspondence secretary
de Robillard, Ainsley — Resident of Ruxley Lane, Ewell
Eldred, Nicholas — Company Secretary of BT Cellnet
Fooks, John — Chairman of Sutton and East Surrey Water
Greer, Nick — Environmental and Planning Manager at Vodafone
Griffiths, Nigel — Company Secretary of Securicor
Hague, the Rt. Hon. William, MP — Leader of Her Majesty's Opposition

Hamilton, the Rt. Hon. Sir Archibald, MP	Member of Parliament for Epsom and Ewell
Harris, Norman	Councillor representing Nork on Reigate and Banstead Borough Council
Haward, A. I.	Honorary Secretary of Nork Residents' Association
Hinton, George	Chairman of Nork Residents' Association
Holder, Phil	Managing Director of Sutton and East Surrey Water
Jones, Dr Sarah	Mast victim and National Trust member
Lansley, Andrew, CBE, MP	Shadow Minister for the Cabinet Office
Litchfield, Doreen	Fellow resident of Lancaster Court
Macfarlane, Sir Neil	Chairman of Securicor
MacLaurin, Lord of Knebworth	Chairman of Vodafone
Modi, Suru	Fellow resident of Lancaster Court
North, Peter	Legal and Estates Services, Resources Department, Reigate and Banstead Borough Council
Philps, Ian	Correspondence Secretary to William Hague
Prescott, the Rt. Hon. John, MP	Deputy Prime Minister and Secretary of State for the Department of the Environment, Transport and the Regions
Redwood, the Rt. Hon. John, MP	Member of Parliament for Wokingham
Ridley, Dr Matt	Writer and contrarian environmentalist
Robinson, Geoffrey	A local resident and former Councillor representing Nork on Reigate and Banstead Borough Council
Sander, G	Resident of Ruxley Lane, Ewell

Selby, Michael	Councillor representing Nork on Reigate and Banstead Borough Council
Smith, Mrs Jean	Councillor representing Ewell Court Ward on Epsom and Ewell Borough Council
Stead, Brian	Councillor representing Nork on Reigate and Banstead Borough Council
Upton, Louisa	Universal Pictorial Press and Agency Ltd.
Vallance, Sir Iain	Chairman, British Telecommunications
Watson, Hamish	Development Control, Environmental Services Department, Reigate and Banstead Borough Council

SUMMARY

1. This book tells the story of a successful campaign to prevent the erection of a Vodafone telecommunication mast just outside my home at Nork, Banstead.
2. Present planning law favours the telecommunications operator at the expense of the householder.
3. We appealed to Council officials, local Councillors, the Residents' Association, our MP, the Prime Minister's office, the Department of the Environment, the Leader of the Opposition and environmental bodies. Several of these failed to reply and none provided effective help.
4. Fighting on grounds of planning law is unlikely to be successful by itself, although it may be a prerequisite for establishing credibility with the real players, the businessmen.
5. In the event we succeeded because we were dealing with a landlord (Sutton and East Surrey Water PLC) who took account of local opinion. That is more than can be said of British Telecommunications PLC.
6. Chapter 8 gives advice on mounting a campaign against telecommunication masts (and other intrusions).
7. Chapter 9 discusses legal reform to redress the present bias of the system against the householder.
8. Proposals for reform have come (among others) from the Council for the Protection of Rural England, Andrew Lansley MP, Friends of the Earth Scotland, John

Corkindale, John Redwood MP, Dr Rolf Bachen and Councillor Jean Smith.

9 There is scope for replacing the present confrontation and overriding of local opposition to masts with market-based solutions in which money changes hands.

10 Permission for masts could be given for a limited period only. In view of the rapid development of telecommunication technology, the need for masts may be ephemeral.

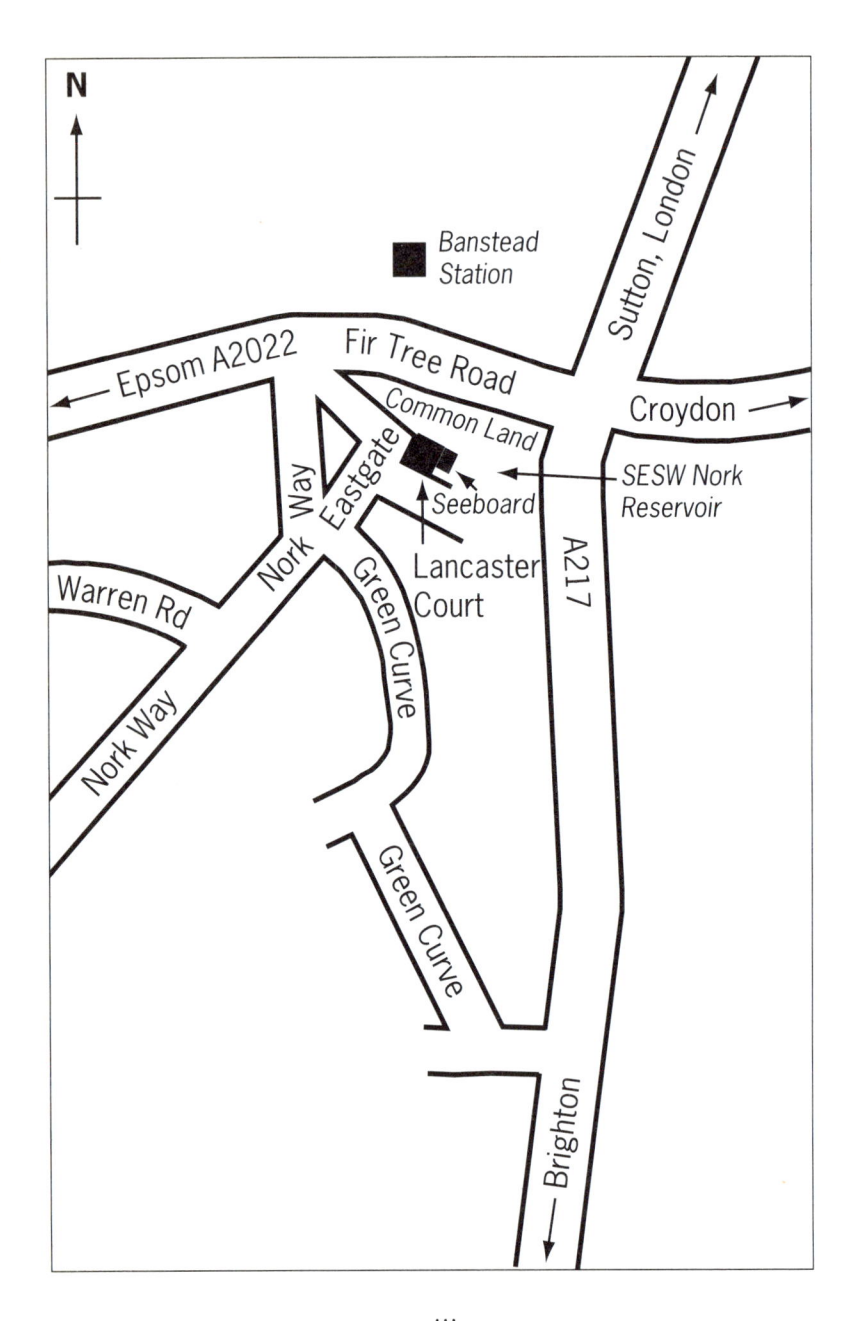

xviii

1

INTRODUCTION

It was on Monday 15 March 1999 that Mary met me outside these flats (Lancaster Court)[1] and said that Vodafone were threatening to put up a telecommunication mast on Sutton and East Surrey Water Company land a few feet from our boundary. Mary lives in the next road, Green Curve, and the first few houses of Green Curve back onto our gardens. She would have been about as near to the mast as we would. She asked whether I would help her in opposing the mast.

I cancelled my engagements for a month and gave the campaign top priority. It was necessary to move quickly, since time was not on our side. It is easier to obstruct the erection of a mast than to get it moved once it is up.

It was an anxious time, although it had its lighter moments. Perhaps I should be grateful to Vodafone for concentrating my mind wonderfully, for getting me out of a rut, for helping me to lose weight, for generating a book that I should not otherwise have written. Or perhaps not.

There is a world of difference between reading about these things in the newspapers and experiencing them yourself. The indifference or hostility that we encountered from the local Council, national politicians and environmental bodies made it clear that we were on our own.

---

[1] Lancaster Court is a few hundred yards to the south west of the crossroads where the A217 London to Brighton crosses the A2022 Epsom to Croydon.

We won without squatting or physical obstruction, without being soaked with rain or dropped on by birds. We won by writing letters. This book explains which letters were effective and which were not. If it gives ideas to others who feel themselves ground down by large companies and remote bureaucrats, so much the better.

2

THE PROBLEM

Vodafone's proposal to erect a mast in Nork Reservoir was the worst threat to these flats (Lancaster Court) since I first came to live here in 1967. For us, as for others threatened with a mast, the problem was threefold.

First, the mast would be an eyesore, clearly visible from many points within the curtilage. In some flats, it would be the first thing the residents saw when they looked out of their windows.

Second, and more important, there is growing concern about the health risks posed by these masts. It is widely believed that the rays they emit could be cancerous or otherwise harmful to health. Perhaps, like smoking, these rays are damaging to some people but not to others. The telecommunication companies say that these risks have not been proved; but they would say that, wouldn't they? The risks have not been disproved either. I did not wish to be proved right by dying of cancer ten years down the line. Remember asbestos. It used to be regarded as a safe substance; but now you must not come into contact with it unless you are dressed like a spaceman.

Third, the value of our flats would in consequence fall and might fall dramatically. I conducted a straw poll of fellow residents to ask whether they would have bought their flats if Vodafone's mast had been there. There were hardly any takers.

Ann is no health freak; but she has strong opinions on a few topics. One is cancerous rays. She doesn't like them. She asked if we could move. I said no. Quite apart from the upheaval, we could not afford to do so. We were financial prisoners in our own home. As it happens, I have bought additional flats over the years, and we live in them as though they made up a house of similar size. I thus had more to lose than my fellow residents, and I was in this sense the right person for Mary to ask for help.

It was clear that the mast would go up if we did nothing. We were bound hand and foot by the legislation; only our tongues were free. We had to make a fuss and to go on doing so until the mast was stopped. We knew that we had much against us, although we were mildly surprised by the indifference, hostility, discourtesy and incompetence that we eventually encountered.

Mary had already been in touch with her brother John. Our first approach must be to Reigate and Banstead Borough Council as the local authority within whose territory Nork Reservoir lies. Planning law is one of John's principal areas of expertise, and Mary already had some background in the subject. There was very little time.

3

THE COUNCIL

Mary had originally learnt of the threat of a mast from a source inside Sutton and East Surrey Water. I shall not identify the source, since a similar leak might be helpful to others fighting masts in future. Mary alerted Geoffrey Robinson, a former Councillor representing Nork on Reigate and Banstead Borough Council. He is a prominent local historian and interested in local affairs. He kindly kept an eye on the planning applications and alerted Mary when the application for the Vodafone mast came through.

The obstacles

The citizen who wishes to oppose the erection of a mast is severely constrained by the primary and secondary legislation of the period 1984–1995.[1] Of the items in the footnote, only the first was primary legislation; all the rest were secondary, which means that the MPs who nominally assented to them were mostly unaware of their existence. Extracts from the legislation

---

[1] The Telecommunications Act 1984; the Town and Country Planning (General Permitted Development) Order 1995 Schedule 2, Part 24; the Telecommunications Prior Approval Procedures Code of Best Practice March 1996 Part 2.1 (ii); PPG8 December 1992 (as amended); Sections 19 and 22 and the General Development Order Consolidation Circular 9/95 Appendix E (June 1995). Vodafone's licence was granted in 1983.

are given in Appendix A. It reads like the product of another era. It is predicated on the assumption that all that matters is a high quality of telecommunication network coverage. There is no role for public opinion or local opposition.

There are four main problems. First, planning permission is not required for masts of 15 metres or less. You need permission for trifling alterations to your home or garden; but a telecommunication company does not need permission to erect a mast outside your back door. Second, the prior approval procedure enables local planning authorities to exercise only limited discretionary control over certain kinds of telecommunication development (in particular, concerning materials, colour, design and siting: see Appendix A). Third, there is no statutory obligation on the Local Authority or anyone else to inform the residents affected; the first they may know of the matter is the sight of an erected mast adjacent to their property. Fourth, the local Planning Authority have only 28 days to make and notify their determination on whether prior approval is required for the siting and appearance of the mast *and* to give or refuse such approval. This period starts as soon as they receive the operator's application for a determination. All four of these were problems for us.

The Councillors

There are three Councillors for Nork on Reigate and Banstead Borough Council – Norman Harris, Michael Selby and Brian Stead, all of whom sit in the political interest of the Residents' Association. As it happens, the Annual General Meeting (AGM) of this Association was held on 15 March, the day Mary broke the news to me about the threat of a mast. I did not go to this meeting; but a fellow resident of these flats, Doreen Litchfield, did. She told me that she had mentioned the matter to Geoffrey Robinson before the meeting; he had said that because of planning laws nothing could be done. She had mentioned the matter to Michael Selby, Chairman of the Borough's Planning Committee, after the meeting; he had merely shrugged his shoulders. She said that no mention of the matter had been made at the Residents' Association AGM; and this has since been confirmed in the report of the AGM in *Nork Quarterly* (Spring 1999, page 5). This made me wonder which residents' interests the Residents' Association was representing and to whom; the Association (of which I am a member) could not have been less concerned with the matter that was uppermost in my mind on the occasion of its AGM.

The application

Vodafone's application to Reigate and Banstead Council (99P/0264) is dated 19 February 1999. The copy I have is date-marked by Reigate and Banstead Council 26 February and 1 March: the post takes a long time to arrive if nobody is really trying. The 28 days apparently started ticking from 26 February; we heard on 25 March that Mr Caseley of the Council's Environmental Services Department was minded to 'terminate' (say yes to Vodafone) that day on the ground that it was much too late to do otherwise. Whose fault was that? 25 March was 27 days after the 26 February date-marking by Reigate and Banstead of the application from Vodafone.

Reigate and Banstead Council did not follow the best practice guidelines published in Section 5, Publicity, of Circular 9/95, 'encouraging publicity so that people likely to be affected can make their views known'. Reigate and Banstead, in the person of Mr Caseley, described as 'Case Officer', also managed to attribute Nork Reservoir to the wrong ward of the borough in the weekly list of planning applications: it was put in Banstead Village ward, which is about a mile to the south east and the other side of the A217.

We know now, but did not know on 15 March, that we had a maximum of ten days to organise local opinion, make representations to local officials and brief local Councillors. We can now see that we were wasting our time. It was in the interest of local officials to save their own backs and do us down, while local Councillors were bystanders.

Mary and I moved into action straight away. John provided as good a legal case for us as was possible in the circumstances. Mary and I contributed several hundred pounds each to his expenses, and he himself was charging less than half his normal fees; so each of us contributed something. Extracts from John's correspondence with Reigate and Banstead Council officials are given in Appendix B. It was a necessary stage in our campaign; but for me the lesson was that the legislation had put us in a hopeless position and that Council officials could always find reasons for turning us down if it was in their interest to do so.

The canvass

Mary and I agreed that we should mobilise local opinion. Fortunately, I had just bought a personal computer for the children and it was easy to run off a circular. The circular explained the background and prepared the way for the collection of signatures to a petition. Doreen Litchfield canvassed these flats (Lancaster Court) on 19 March, and I canvassed the flats opposite (Eastgate) and ten or more roads nearby on Saturday 20 March and over the weekend. Mary was working part-time throughout this period, so I was willing to do most of the legwork; I was much assisted by Ann and Suru Modi and other helpers. Appendix C is a copy of the circular of 20 March.

I was anxious to get the job done and thus not to engage in unnecessary conversations; but some discussion was inevitable. This must be the most thorough canvass of opinion on this subject that has ever been undertaken in the area. All the talk I had on the subject was civil and most was friendly. Opinion among those I spoke to was more than ten to one in favour of what I was doing, often passionately so. This was true of mobile phone users and non-users alike. Most of the people I spoke to were against further masts on any terms and were willing to tolerate imperfections, if any, in transmission and reception. It was notable that there was no diminution of support as I moved away from Nork Reservoir: for example, there was just as much opposition to the mast at the west end of Warren Road as at the east end. I even canvassed the other side of the two local main roads (to the east of the A217 from London to Brighton, and to the north of the A2022 from Epsom to Croydon): there too, opinion was just as hostile to the mast as it was at Lancaster Court and Eastgate.

What would have happened if a representative of Vodafone had undertaken a similar canvass? Well, he might have been lynched, which would have helped to clear his mind and brief him and his company on local opinion. Unfortunately, the companies, politicians and bureaucrats who are so keen to bombard other people with these rays are no keener to take first-hand soundings of public opinion on the subject than they are to expose themselves to the bombardment.

One conversation made a deep impression on me. A woman in Dunnymans Road, to the east of the A217, said that she agreed profoundly with what I was doing, but she would not support me, because she was afraid that the mast would be moved nearer to *her* home. I had never looked at this matter in the perspective of NIMBY (not in my backyard); and what she said made me determined to fight for the interests of her neighbours in Dunnymans Road and nearby as much as for Lancaster Court. I was honour-bound to do so. This attitude distinguished me from some of the other players in the drama, who would have counted it a success to have had the mast moved a few yards towards the A217; I am not naming them, since the outcome has been satisfactory.

We collected 124 signatures urging Reigate and Banstead Council to do everything possible to prevent the installation of the Vodafone mast in Nork Reservoir. I delivered the original of this petition by hand to Michael Selby on Monday 22 March and had a formal acknowledgement from him on 23 March.

By 25 March, Reigate and Banstead Council had received 106 letters on the subject. Letters are perceived as counting more on these occasions than signatures, since some people will sign anything to get rid of a petitioner on the doorstep.

Correspondence with Caseley and Cowle

I had meanwhile written on 20 March to Mr Caseley of Reigate and Banstead Environmental Services Department, copying to him letters of the same date to Vodafone and Sutton and East Surrey Water. As I had had no reply from Councillors or their officials and understood that a decision was to be made on the evening of 25 March, I wrote on that day to Brian Cowle, Mayor Elect of Reigate and Banstead, and delivered the letter by hand; it is reproduced as Appendix D. Brian Cowle lived until recently in Green Curve, a few yards from Mary, so he should have had enough local background to understand the problem; but he was apparently preoccupied with his role as Mayor Elect, and I have never had a reply or acknowledgement.

The Planning Committee

The matter was considered at a meeting of the Reigate and Banstead Council Planning Committee on the evening of 25 March. Councillor Michael Selby (he of the shrugging shoulders) was in the Chair. The planning application worksheet speaks of 'a petition signed by 106 residents of Nork and Banstead'; but there are 124 signatures on my photocopy of the original which I delivered to Selby's home on 22 March. The worksheet also speaks of '89 individual letters ... objecting to this proposal'; this is also an understatement, as I heard from another source that the number of letters received exceeded 100. As far as I know, this was by far the highest level of objection to a mast that Reigate and Banstead had ever received; and it had been achieved over a period of ten days, from 15 to 25 March.

The Committee spent nearly 30 minutes discussing the proposal. They concluded: 'There is a need for this unit to enhance the existing coverage at the Banstead crossroad junction (including increased capacity).' But who says there is a need? It was not the message I received when canvassing in Nork. Mobile phone users and non-users alike, my respondents were more than ten to one against having a mast on any terms and regarded the rectification of imperfections (if any) in the coverage as less important than the many benefits of not having a mast. The Committee also concluded that: 'the siting and design of this pole unit are such that it would not be obtrusive to adjoining residents or to the semi-rural landscape of this treed part of Banstead'. That is not the opinion of the residents; it is the opinion of non-residents deciding our fate at a meeting miles away in Reigate. Councillor Selby said, 'OK [reluctantly]'; but a reluctant OK is still an OK. The only stipulation was that the mast should be painted green, not red.

My interpretation of events is that Reigate and Banstead officials first kept us in the dark and then, when we found out through our own initiative, fought us rather than Vodafone: we only pay their salaries. The Councillors did nothing to help, or nothing effective. During the afternoon of 25 March a messenger from the Council delivered to my home a blank form entitled 'Reigate and Banstead Borough Council Complaints Procedure: your right to complain'; and in the whole of this sorry business this was the one thing the Council got right. In the event, despite what I said to Brian Cowle (Appendix D), I did not complain to the local ombudsman; it would have been a waste of time even to obtain a judgement in my favour, when the priority was to win the battle.

A main reason why the Councillors were political neuters in these proceedings is that at Reigate and Banstead, as elsewhere, officials are accepting or rejecting proposals for masts under powers delegated to them by the Council. In an inversion of normal democratic procedures, Councillors have to make representations to their own officials, who then take the decisions. The Nork Residents' Association Committee Report to the AGM 1999 said: 'Our Councillors ... reported to us various concerns at how business was increasingly being taken out of the hands of elected members and decisions being [sic] taken by officers on their behalf' (*Nork Quarterly*, Spring 1999, page 7).

Waverley Council

Reigate and Banstead may not be the worst local Council at handling applications for masts. The Eagle Radio Network News broadcast the following on 17 April: 'Farnham residents are stunned after a mistake by Waverley Council has left them living in the shadow of a 50 foot telecom mast. Officials had been planning to refuse permission when Cellnet notified the Council of its plans – but due to a so-called administrative error they forgot to do it in time, which according to the law means the mobile phone company can go ahead to put up the free-standing mast without notifying neighbours. Red-faced Councillors had 28 days to turn down the application for the tower, but they refused consent 2 days late.'

But at least Waverley Council was planning to refuse permission for the mast, which is more than can be said for Reigate and Banstead.

The local press

The behaviour of the local press shows an interesting pattern. The former Epsom, Banstead and Leatherhead *Informer* reported our campaign on the front page of its issue of 25 March, the day Reigate and Banstead decided to let Vodafone's application through. Mary and her husband Ian were quoted by name. The *Banstead Herald* did not use material we sent (although on 10 February they had given 15 column inches to a fight against an Orange tower at Chipstead Golf Club; Reigate and Banstead received five letters of objection to this tower and a petition with 19 signatures, way below our figures). What they did publish on 7 April, 13 days after the determination of the application on 25 March, was a report headlined 'New Mast Makes Residents See Red' and starting: 'Residents of an exclusive block of flats have seen red about a green-painted 15-metre mobile telephone mast being put up near their homes. Flat-dwellers in Lancaster Court, Nork, have sent a 100-name petition to Reigate and Banstead Council objecting to the mast...'

The report cites a spokesman for Reigate and Banstead Council, and this snide and misleading wording reads like a plant from one of their officials in an attempt to present us in an unsympathetic light. Even the estate agents do not call us exclusive, and the 124 signatures (not 100) to the petition did not come from Lancaster Court (where fewer than 100 people live) but from about a dozen roads over a wide area.[2]

The officials

Appendix B gives extracts from the correspondence between John and the Council officials in the spring of 1999. It illustrates the obstacles to defeating a mast through ordinary procedures. The resident is bound hand and foot by the legislation. Council officials have every incentive to fight the residents who are obliged by law to pay their salaries and are unable to vote them out of office. They have no incentive to fight the telecommunication operators who have deep pockets and can make life uncomfortable for officials who oppose them, by going to appeal. The officials followed their own interests by supporting Vodafone against us and made life as difficult for us as possible by keeping us in the dark. The expression 'given resources' implies that they could not afford a postage stamp or telephone call to let us know what was going on, which is pretty rich from a bunch of officials who have recently built themselves a large and unnecessary new office block. It is of little consequence whether or not the Borough Council 'purported to accept the proposal in environmental terms' when the Director of Environmental Services concluded that 'no resident had been disadvantaged' by a mast 35 metres from his home.

The assessment that a Vodafone mast at Nork Reservoir would disadvantage no resident of this remote outpost of

---

[2]The *Banstead Herald* treated us more favourably later. Catherine O'Mara gave advance notice of the present book in a report headed 'Protesting doctor pens a mast piece' (19 April 2000).

Reigate's empire was not confirmed by my canvass of local opinion. The reaction was one of outrage, a mixture of anger and disbelief, although a number of my better-informed respondents recognised that this was indeed the situation that had been inflicted on the householders by the politicians.

4

THE RESIDENTS' ASSOCIATION

A Bishop was visiting an old people's home in the course of his pastoral duties. 'Do you know who I am?' he asked a resident. 'No, I don't,' came the answer; 'but don't worry: Matron will tell you.'

A similar identity crisis seems to afflict Residents' Associations. They are neither fish nor flesh nor good red herring. They are voluntary bodies whose policies and interests may conflict with those of non-members and indeed of members. When they stand in local elections as a political interest, they are by definition working against the interests of other parties. Their activities may or may not have the support of those they purport to represent. They may crowd out others who are more closely in touch with local opinion. But they have a great attraction for elements of the local press and for businessmen seeking to impose their wishes on a local population: they can purport to represent local opinion and thus save others the trouble of finding out what the locals really think. The Roman Emperor Caligula was reported to have wished that the people of Rome had only one neck, so that he could cut off the head once and for all: a Roman Residents' Association could have been the answer to his prayers.

In the matter of telecommunication masts, not all Residents' Associations have won local plaudits. In a letter to the *Epsom Informer* of 4 March 1999, G. Sander of Ruxley Lane, Ewell, thanked 'The Informer and those other residents who have acted on this matter, something that the [Epsom and Ewell] Residents' Association and Council have failed dismally to do.'[1]

The Nork Residents' Association and its Councillors, in their various capacities and wearing their various hats, did veto a proposal by Vodafone (received by Reigate and Banstead on 22 March 1999) to erect a telecommunication mast in Nork Park (see page 35). But, since Nork Park is the property of Reigate and Banstead Council, it would have required the incompetence of Waverley Council (see Waverley Council, page 12) to let this application through. Even Reigate and Banstead shot this sitting duck. Where applications were made to erect masts on the land of other owners, it was another story.

George Hinton, Chairman of Nork Residents' Association, wrote to the Chief Executive of Sutton and East Surrey Water PLC (SESW) about the Nork Reservoir mast shortly after the determination of Reigate and Banstead in Vodafone's favour on 25 March. My copy of his letter is dated 27 March. He expressed concern that local residents were not informed of the application; referred to more than 100 letters of objection submitted to the Council's planning department in a very limited time; noted the huge swell of anger about the placing of the pole on SESW land; asked SESW, as a responsible landowner and neighbour, to give the residents an adequate hearing to express their views; and asked for a delay in proceeding with this construction to avoid unnecessary confrontation. This letter was quick off the mark and useful as far as it went; but how far did it go? George Hinton sent me a copy of this letter on 31 March, saying that it might be more constructive (than opposing the mast at Nork Reservoir) to ask Reigate's Director of Planning if he had considered recommending that Vodafone first investigate the possibilities of sharing other masts in the

---

[1] A more favourable picture of Residents' Associations and their Councillors is provided by the activities of Councillor Jean Smith, who sits on Epsom and Ewell Borough Council in the interest of the Residents' Association. She was elected to Surrey County Council in November 1999. See Chapter 7 and Appendix R. The Nork Residents' Association and its officers have done good work in other contexts, notably by frustrating the intention of 'travellers' to occupy land in Nork Park; for example, *Nork Quarterly*, Summer 2000, page 9.

immediate area: 'Another cellphone provider, Securicor, has recently stated an intent to erect a mast on the premises of Banstead Builders' Merchants at Banstead Station. Vodafone ought to be able to negotiate a sharing agreement to use this mast rather than erect another within 2–300 metres?' This idea did not appeal to me, first, because there was no reason to believe that Reigate and Banstead officials would change their previous attitude towards residents of this area and, second, because we are not much further from Banstead Station than we are from Nork Reservoir: my purpose was to get the Vodafone mast out of Nork, not to move it to another site which would be nearer to somebody else.

The late Lord Home remarked about an operation he underwent that the surgeons were attempting the impossible, to put backbone into a politician. I was attempting to put backbone into the Nork Residents' Association and its representatives by means of the activities described in Chapter 6. In a circular of 13 April, A. I. Haward, Honorary Secretary of the Association, said that the Association were negotiating on 'two proposals outstanding, one near Banstead Station and one at Nork Reservoir'. In a letter to me of 24 April, Councillor Norman Harris said: 'I am hoping to speak to the Managing Director of SESW early next week for a final decision on the Nork Reservoir site.' This was alarming news: the same man said in the same letter: 'My personal opinion of sites in and around Nork has always been the same. We do not want them, however as the law stands the Council can only stop them if they are on our land.' What would this man concede? Fortunately, Mary was also meeting Phil Holder, Managing Director of SESW, and in a letter of 17 May she told me: 'I have urged that the mast should be moved right off the site.'

When he learnt of my approaches to Vodafone and SESW (see Chapter 6) Councillor Harris asked me to tone down my activities. 'Softly softly catchee monkey,' he said. Not so: in situations of this kind, understatement is not an option. There is a short, sharp expression for what softly softly catchee. Come to think of it, there are four such short, sharp expressions, differing subtly in detail but conveying in their various ways the same unmistakable message.

One area where the Residents' Association could not fairly be accused of understatement is joining a campaign when the work had been done by others. I refer to the activities of Councillor Harris as campaign coordinator in Chapter 6.

5

THE POLITICIANS: BUCKPASSERS UNITED

It was never likely that we would receive much practical help from the politicians: it was they who had got us into this mess. Nevertheless, the campaign was throwing up questions of public policy, and it was possible that we might benefit indirectly if these questions could be brought to the attention of senior politicians.

Vodafone's application to Reigate and Banstead was determined (passed) on 25 March. I had already written to my MP, Archie Hamilton, on 23 March and to the Prime Minister and the Secretary of State for the Environment on 24 March.

The Rt. Hon. Sir Archibald Hamilton, MP

Archie Hamilton is a busy and prominent man, and I do not like to trouble him with my petty concerns, especially as he knows me personally. I have therefore approached him only a few times over the years, about matters of personal or public importance. On most or all of these occasions his response has been to send on my letter to the appropriate Government Minister or other dignitary and, when he had the dignitary's reply, to send it on to me without comment (let alone commitment to anything). This method of dealing with constituents must have helped to conserve his time for weightier matters. I did not therefore expect earth-shaking results from writing to him about the Vodafone mast; and so I was not disappointed. My letter to him of 23 March 1999 is reproduced as Appendix E.

He wrote the same day to John Fooks, Chairman of Sutton and East Surrey Water. He has not so far responded to the fourth and fifth paragraphs of my letter, the ones about the responsibility of the previous Conservative Government for the legislation from which we were now suffering.[1]

The reply to his letter of 23 March to John Fooks, Chairman of SESW, was dated 26 March and came from Phil Holder, Managing Director. Archie Hamilton sent it on to me without comment. This reply contained three points of interest. First, it said: 'The rent we receive from masts has played no part in the policy we have adopted. However, when a mast is to be located on our land we require that the proper rent is paid.' This is the neatest example of eating your cake and having it that I have come across for years. Second, it said: 'We have decided that our approach should be to leave the decision as to whether or not there should be a mast to the local council which has been elected to represent the interests of the residents.' I have described above just how Reigate and Banstead had been 'representing the interests of the residents' in this matter. For a body which by its own account has many telecommunication masts on its sites, it is notable how little SESW knew about the legal and political process governing their erection. The local Council had not taken a 'decision as to whether or not there should be a mast'; it had limited grounds on which to refuse or amend an application. And decisions were not taken by those 'elected to represent the interests of the residents' but by officials who had not been elected by anyone. Third, the letter said that I and many of my neighbours use mobile phones and treated this as a clinching argument for erecting the mast; but if the mobile phone users themselves were campaigning against the mast, whom was it intended to benefit?

Archie Hamilton sent on some technical material from the

---

[1] In a letter of 18 January 2000 he said: 'I believe that the thinking was that, if local people were allowed to object, then very few masts would ever go up, and it would take an interminable time for the country to have a well-developed network'. No wonder the Conservatives were so heavily defeated at the 1997 General Election.

Department of the Environment and wished me the best of luck with the campaign (which was more forthcoming than usual); but I did not manage to interest him in the political background to the problem and the political possibilities inherent in its solution. (See paragraphs four and following of Appendix E.)

Cabinet Ministers

I wrote to the Prime Minister, Tony Blair, on 24, 25, 26 and 27 March. All the letters were sent by Royal Mail Special Delivery (express post). He has been keen to blackguard his predecessors, and I thought there was a chance that this material might catch the eye of someone in his office as a means of putting right what they had done wrong. Some hope.

These four letters are reproduced as Appendices F–I. Appendix G notes the inconsistencies in Vodafone's Notice of Intention to Reigate and Banstead Council: if local residents were deeply hostile to the installation and motorists would be criminally reckless to use their mobiles in the area, just whom was the improved coverage intended to benefit?

I had a reply dated 26 March from Mrs J. Crawley, The Prime Minister's correspondence secretary. Mr Blair had asked that my letter (24 March?) be forwarded to the Department of Environment, Transport and the Regions (DETR) 'so that they may reply to you direct'. I had also written (by express post) to John Prescott, the Secretary of State, in terms identical to those of Appendices F–I.

The Prime Minister's hope that the DETR would reply to me direct on his behalf was not to be realised. They did not reply directly or indirectly, on his behalf or their own or anyone else's. Perhaps the reason was that the Secretary of State was busy at the time snorkelling in the Far East in the course of his Ministerial duties, a colourful detail that gives a new meaning to the old saying 'socialism is the language of priorities' (or is it 'the language of priorities is the religion of socialism'?). But it is apparently DETR policy not to answer letters from the public anyway: this is my own experience (four letters out of four), and it has since been corroborated from other sources.

I wrote to the Prime Minister on 30 March thanking him for Mrs Crawley's letter but pointing out that Mr de Robillard had not heard from John Prescott about the mast at Ruxley Lane, Ewell (see Chapter 7) over a period of three months and that this leisurely timescale was not adequate to the emergency. I had no reply. Buckpassers of the world, unite: you have nothing to lose but your correspondents.

However, I *did* get a reply from the office of William Hague.

The Rt. Hon. William Hague, MP

I had written to the Prime Minister drawing his attention to what I believed was a potential vote-winner. In the interest of the political impartiality for which I am well known to my friends, I thought I should perform the same service for William Hague. I wrote to him on 29 March enclosing the letters of 20 March to Vodafone, SESW and Reigate and Banstead Council and also the letters of 24, 25, 26 and 27 March to the Prime Minister. I said: 'The letter of 27 March suggests that a policy of restricting the installation of telecommunication masts could be a political vote-winner. I should not like to make this suggestion to the Prime Minister without also making it to you.' I concluded: 'I should like to record my thanks to Sir Archibald Hamilton for his support.' My letter to William Hague amounted to 86 words spread over three paragraphs and nine lines. The reply of 6 April from Ian Philps, correspondence secretary to the Leader of the Opposition, is a collector's item.

Mr Hague had asked him to thank me for my recent letter and to reply on his behalf. He was grateful to me for drawing this matter to his attention. However, whilst he (Philps) had no wish to appear unhelpful, he was afraid that the office (of the Leader of the Opposition) could not intervene in such cases. As I ought to know, there was a strict convention in the House of Commons that prevented an MP from becoming involved in matters affecting another Member's constituent. All he could suggest was that I should, if I had not already done so, get in touch with my own Member of Parliament. He was sorry he could not give a more positive response.

The mind boggles. Belief is beggared. Ian Philps must hold a record for the world's shortest attention span. Not only had he apparently not looked at any of my seven supporting letters; but the 86 words of my letter to William Hague were too testing a challenge. Where he makes any contact with what I said, he manages to get everything upside down, back to front and inside out. He suggests that I get in touch with my own Member of Parliament (which I had explained I had already done). He is 'afraid that this office cannot intervene in cases of this kind'; it had never occurred to me that it could or should. The whole purpose of my writing to William Hague was explained in the second paragraph of my letter: 'The letter [to the Prime Minister] of 27 March suggests that a policy of restricting the installation of telecommunication masts could be a political vote-winner. I should not like to make this suggestion to the Prime Minister without also making it to you.' But there are a lot of long words and difficult concepts in these two sentences; not everyone can be expected to cope with material like this.

I wrote to William Hague again in December 1999 enclosing a draft of Chapter 5 of the present book which was substantially identical to the published version. Ian Philps replied: 'We have carefully noted your further comments. As the leader of the Conservative Party, Mr Hague fully appreciates the vital need to reflect long and hard on the views of people such as yourself.' So my last communication seems to have gone into the bin unread, just like its predecessor.

My first reaction on reading the letters from Ian Philps was: with clowns like this in his office, it is no wonder that William Hague has been in trouble. On further consideration, this may be simplistic and unfair to Ian Philps. Maybe he is just an official playing a humble but conscientious part in an Orwellian conspiracy against the country's citizens (or, as I prefer to call them, the Queen's subjects).

Time was, and not so long ago, when you could expect a reply if you wrote to a Government Department. Your letter might be ill drafted, factually wrong, off the point or at variance with Government policy; but at least someone would read it and write back. The reply might be evasive, economical with the truth or downright dishonest; but at least you got a reply. You could then have another go. Your further effort elicited a further reply. Eventually one of the two corresponding parties collapsed through exhaustion, usually the Government; but at least somebody in Government had taken note of what you said, even if Government policy had not.

Happy but distant days! It is all very different now. I have never known a time when it was more difficult to get through to anybody – Government or Opposition, Conservative or Labour, MP or non-MP. This is a problem going beyond telecommunication masts. The dominant influences are now focus groups, spin doctors, public relations consultants and the like: for Labour and Conservatives alike, the effect of these people is to make it very difficult to get through, even with an important message, let alone to get anything done. 'Mr Blair hopes you will understand that, as the matter you raise is the responsibility of Environment, Transport and the Regions, he has asked that your letter be forwarded to that Department so that they may reply to you direct on his behalf.' They didn't. 'All I can suggest is that you should, if you have not already done so, get in touch with your own Member of Parliament. I am sorry I cannot give a more positive response.' I share the regret of Ian Philps that he could not give a more positive response. It may not be entirely his fault.

As local Councillors and officials of the Reigate and Banstead Council were indifferent or hostile to our interests and it was practically impossible to get through to anybody in Government or Opposition (especially as our present MP had helped to pass the legislation that caused the trouble), then we had to abandon political protest as totally inadequate to the situation and concentrate on the business interests involved.

6

THE BUSINESSMEN

On 27 March, two days after Reigate and Banstead determined against us, Mary and I had a word about tactics. Reigate and Banstead officials and councillors and the national politicians had already turned us down or were in the course of doing so. We were running out of options. Mary said that our best plan was to put pressure on Sutton and East Surrey Water, and I agreed. Mary also mentioned the possibility of going to a more expensive firm of lawyers and continuing to fight the mast on grounds of planning law and the like. I thought that this would be expensive and ineffective: we had already done our best on this terrain, and I did not believe that we would be more successful in future. Mary agreed. Mary had to spend more time at work and I said that I would start handling dealings with SESW. However, we would keep in touch with each other and not make significant new moves without prior notice.

As I saw it, there were three elements in our approach to SESW. First, I would try to mount a letter-writing campaign like the one against Reigate and Banstead Council. Second, I would ensure that the arguments, as well as the strength of feeling, against the intended mast were brought to the attention of SESW. Third, and as a result of the first two, I would try to guard against the risk of Nork residents being represented by wimps or quislings in any discussions or negotiations with SESW.

I intended also to pursue correspondence with Vodafone,

although I recognised that they were likely to be a hard and unsympathetic crew. As one of the largest quoted companies in the country, they do not have to take account of non-financial opinion. Their idea of public relations is sponsoring the Derby. SESW might be a softer touch. As a privatised utility, they had to take account of public opinion. Their twice-yearly bills were accompanied by free handouts explaining what good citizens they were and how much help they gave to the Third World. Again, Nork residents were all SESW customers.

It takes two to tango. The mast could not go up unless both Vodafone and SESW wished it to do so. If either pulled out, we were free. The purpose of the campaign was the same for both companies: to penetrate the corporate carapace and persuade senior management that life would be more comfortable and agreeable for them if the mast did not go up than if it did (or, to put the same thing differently, that if the mast did go up, their lives might be uncomfortable and disagreeable). Some have more natural talent for this kind of representation than others. Partly by chance and partly by design, Mary and I worked a variant of Spenlow and Jorkins. Readers of *David Copperfield* will remember that Spenlow was a hard man who pretended to be a softie compelled to be hard by the intransigent Jorkins in the background. Mary is far too pleasant and agreeable to be a natural Spenlow; but it was convenient to have me in the background, not participating in meetings but ensuring that the right message got through to the businessmen.

The campaign

I had already written on 20 March to John Fooks, Chairman of Sutton and East Surrey Water PLC (see Appendix J) and Lord MacLaurin of Knebworth, Chairman of Vodafone (see Appendix K). I wrote to them again on Tuesday 23 March reporting the 124 signatures that we had collected over the weekend. The letter of 23 March to Lord MacLaurin was acknowledged by David Channing Williams, Managing Director, who said that he had passed my letter to Nick Greer; the acknowledgement was sent by second-class post, which was notable in the circumstances. The two letters to John Fooks were acknowledged on 26 March by P. B. Holder, Managing Director of SESW, who attached a copy of the letter of 26 March from John Fooks to Sir Archibald Hamilton (discussed in Chapter 5).

I did not take up the offer to speak to Phil Holder on the telephone. Throughout this affair, I had no meetings or telephone conversations with representatives of SESW or Vodafone.

Although I was writing to both SESW and Vodafone in similar terms and most of my letters to one of these companies were copied or faxed to the other, SESW had priority as the target of letters from residents. All residents were SESW customers and SESW had, at least nominally, a concern for its public image. I ran this campaign in two stages. First, on 27 March I circulated a leaflet to the 124 signatories of the petition to Reigate and Banstead Council: they should be sympathisers and already briefed, and I had their names and addresses. Second, on 28 March (Palm Sunday) I circulated a leaflet to residents of Nork Way, Warren Road, Fir Tree Road and elsewhere; this is reproduced as Appendix L. We made sure we had plenty of ink and paper, and my children Christina and Timothy ran off hundreds of leaflets on the new personal computer.

I understand that the leaflets generated more than 100 letters to SESW. Some dozens were copied to me. Several correspondents wondered why SESW were so bothered about the Third World if they ignored the wishes and interests of customers a few feet from Nork Reservoir. Once again, distance did not lend enchantment: opposition was as strong a mile away from Nork Reservoir as it was in the front line.

I did what I had asked so many others to do and wrote again to Phil Holder on 28 March (see Appendix M).

By good fortune, the *Sunday Telegraph* was at this time running a series of sardonic cartoons in the business section on the theme of businessmen behaving badly. I was getting further and further behind with reading the newspapers; but I did manage to look at the business section each Sunday. The cartoon on 28 March was a gift; I recaptioned it and sent a copy to Phil Holder (see Appendix N).

Nick Greer, Environmental and Planning Manager at Vodafone, wrote to me on 29 March. He had raised my concerns with his colleagues responsible for this site and would contact me following thorough discussions with them as to the site selection process undertaken as well as the other issues which I had raised. In addition, he could confirm that the intended physical development of the site had been put on hold until he had had the opportunity personally to inspect the site to ensure that the correct procedures had been followed. He would write again following his visit to the site. This was much the most polite and helpful letter that I had received on the subject from anyone on the other side; but it did not preclude his writing again to say that he had visited the site, that he was satisfied that everything was in order and that the mast was going up the following day.

So far, the only communication of substance that I had received from SESW was a copy of the off-the-point form letter from John Fooks to Sir Archibald Hamilton. There was no sign of yielding there. Moreover, one or two voices in the residents' camp were sympathetic to the idea of moving the mast nearer to the A217, which was precisely what the woman in Dunnymans Road was so keen to avoid. Word had reached me of impending discussions between SESW and parties purporting to represent Nork residents. I was alarmed that someone might accept with gratitude some trifling concession from SESW. It was time to write to John Fooks again, which I did by fax on 30 March (see Appendix O).

The letter of 29 March from Nick Greer suggested that, against all expectations, Vodafone might be less hard-line than SESW. Had the company a soft side behind that rugged exterior? It was worth a try. I would appeal to the Chairman. After all, erecting unwanted masts in the teeth of fierce local opposition is not how a peer behaves. *Noblesse Oblige*. It is just not cricket.

I felt that my prose might need enlivening with more visual aids. I remembered that Louisa Upton, the daughter of an old army friend, worked for Universal Pictorial Press and Agency Ltd in London. I gave her a ring. Had Universal any photographs of Lord MacLaurin? Yes, they had, and she described them to me. Moreover, Universal had copyright and I was free to use the photograph of my choice, subject to far-from-onerous conditions and the payment of a modest fee. I went to London on the morning of 1 April for the sole purpose of collecting the photograph. I had already decided which one I wanted, and when I saw it for the first time I was not disappointed. It was reproduced in Nork and District Residents' *Vodafone Newsletter No. 1* (see page 30). I was right about visual aids: my commentary does its best, but a picture is worth a thousand words.

I got back from London at 11.30 and composed the commentary, which Ann typed. Costa did the artwork and improved enormously on anything Ann and I could have done between us. The *Newsletter* was faxed to Lord MacLaurin, John Fooks and Phil Holder at 3.00. I wanted them to have this Easter greeting in good time, with the long weekend to think it over.

The photograph shows Lord MacLaurin on the occasion of his introduction in the House of Lords. Louisa tells me that this ceremony is for peers of new creation, succeeding hereditary peers not being new peers in this sense. I am sorry I could not be there. '*Then follows the new peer with two peers of his own rank as supporters or sponsors, the junior in front and the senior behind him. The new peer and his supporters carry cocked hats in their left hands and wear parliamentary robes... Garter now conducts the new peer and his supporters to the bench appropriate to their degree, where at Garter's direction they sit, put on their hats, rise, and bow to the Chancellor three times...*' and more to this effect (Information Sheet No. 1: The Ceremony of Introduction in the House of Lords, July 1986).

Call me old-fashioned, but it is heartbreaking to compare this glory with the pared-down, cool-Britannia version introduced by a modernising Government. For those with a strong stomach, the new ceremony is described in 'The Introduction of New Members to the House of Lords, June 1998'. Introduction *to*? I thought it was Introduction *in*. Is nothing

Fax to: Lord MacLaurin of Knebworth   01635-522835
Fax copies to: Mr John Fooks and Mr. P. B. Holder   01737-766807
    01883-627792
By hand to: Councillor Norman Harris
               Mr. George Hinton
Further distribution on hold for the time.

NORK AND DISTRICT RESIDENTS' VODAFONE NEWSLETTER NO. 1
1 April 1999

CAN THIS MAN BE OUR SAVIOUR?

Nork residents appeal to Lord MacLaurin of Knebworth

Residents of Nork, Banstead, fearing that Mr. John Fooks, Chairman of Sutton and East Surrey Water PLC, may still allow the erection of a Vodafone mast at Nork reservoir, are carrying their protest higher up the social scale.

They are appealing to the good nature of Lord MacLaurin of Knebworth, Chairman of Vodafone, as well as his regard for the commercial interests of his company.

If they are rebuffed by Lord MacLaurin, they are considering other possibilities, any of which could be of interest to the Press.

Lord MacLaurin of Knebworth.
Formerly Mr. Ian Carter MacLaurin.

'My pet hate: people who are scruffy and don't present themselves well'
Lord MacLaurin of Knebworth, May 1999

sacred? These modernisers are even attacking the nation's prepositions.

Although I do not agree with Lord MacLaurin about everything and may even have had a tilt with him about Nork Reservoir (or should it be a joust with a nobleman?), I am glad that the present degenerate days of plastic and tinfoil had not engulfed the House of Lords when he was introduced. His introduction was 'appropriate to his degree'.

I asked Louisa whether Universal had any photographs of Lady Thatcher on her introduction in the House of Lords (similar to the ceremony for Lord MacLaurin except that 'women peers wear a tricorne hat ... women peers do not remove their hats'). Louisa said that they had not: Lady Thatcher had had her own photographs taken, possibly because she did not wish to lose control of copyright. Not for the first time, I was impressed by Lady Thatcher's attention to detail.

The date of 1 April on *Vodafone Newsletter No. 1* was not intended to signify anything. We were working to a timetable imposed on us by others. I just wanted to get a message of good cheer into the offices of those concerned by Easter. If the date of the *Newsletter* had some unintended significance, that was not my doing.

Louisa told me that it would be in order to circulate a limited number of the Nork and District Residents' *Vodafone Newsletter No. 1* without infringing Universal's restrictions. Thirty copies may have been mentioned, but no matter. Nothing was distributed to anyone in Nork except Mary and Ann. The only other recipients were MacLaurin, Fooks, Holder, Harris and Hinton. The purpose of the *Newsletter* was to alert these gentlemen to the state of opinion here. There was no need to circulate to the residents, who were already aware of the problem.

Although I had had a polite letter from Nick Greer, I still had not heard from Lord MacLaurin. By contrast, as it happened, I was in correspondence at this time with Dr David Hope, Archbishop of York, on a literary matter that had nothing to do with telecommunication masts. Dr Hope was kind enough to write to me himself, answering my question perfectly. I could not help wondering: has Lord MacLaurin a smaller private office to help him with his correspondence? And is he a busier man than Dr Hope? Or has he just a short attention span?[1]

In *Tiger by the Tail*[2] Lord MacLaurin describes his maiden speech in the House of Lords. He was advised that the essential requirements were humour and humility. 'Just before I started to speak Margaret Thatcher came in and took the seat immediately in front of me. As if I wasn't humble enough already.' No, sir, you were not. 'Remember that the most important person in the organisation is the most humble. Acknowledge them and say thank you – it doesn't take two seconds and it's very important.'[3] It is a pity that this respect for the downtrodden has not extended to neighbours of your masts. You could have abased yourself still further and communicated with them.

I admire Lord MacLaurin for his toughness of character. He clearly belongs to the old school: stiff upper lip, never explain, never apologise. However, for a captain of the communications industry, he seemed to be remarkably deaf. I wondered at times whether I should send him an old-fashioned ear trumpet. Fortunately the *Sunday Telegraph* provided one on Easter Sunday, 4 April. Their cartoon of this date, recaptioned by us 'This is how Vodafone treats a resident protesting against a Vodafone mast' is reproduced in Appendix P. The artwork was done by Costa Sarafoglou of Bespoke Designs, appearing as Mr John Smith of Artful Plans Ltd. The cartoon was sent to Lord MacLaurin on 7 April under cover of my letter of that date (Appendix P). Thoughtful as ever, I sent a copy to John Fooks.

Despite what John Fooks had said in his letter of 26 March to Sir Archibald Hamilton, I wondered whether it was really

---

[1]Lord MacLaurin has described his 'least favourite personal characteristic' as 'a short attention span when things clearly don't interest me' (interview with Carol Kennedy, *The Director*, May 1999.) I would not disagree with this assessment. It is clear that the damage done by his masts to their neighbours does not interest Lord MacLaurin. Other helpful advice from the same source includes: 'Stay very close to your customers, so that you deliver what they want'. *Customers*, not neighbours, although some of his neighbours were customers as well.
[2]Macmillan, 1999, pages 153 and following. The title was earlier used in *Tiger by the Tail: The Keynesian Legacy of Inflation*, essays compiled and introduced by Sudha R. Shenoy (Institute of Economic Affairs, London, Hobart Paperback No. 4, 1978).
[3]Interview with Carol Kennedy, *The Director*, May 1999.

true of SESW that 'the rent we receive from masts has played no part in the policy we have adopted'. Would his shareholders be pleased if this were so? The place for these otherworldly sentiments is the monastery or the hermitage rather than the boardroom. But, just in case John Fooks might have the occasional moment of mercenary weakness, I played the devil's part and tried to tempt him with money.

15 April 1999

Dear Sir,

Nork Reservoir telecommunications apparatus

I understand that the fee paid to landowners by companies like Vodafone for permission to erect a mast is in the order of £3,000 - £5,000 a year.

In order to prevent SESW's losing financially from behaving as a good neighbour, I am willing to treat this fee as ransom money and match Vodafone's latest bid with this price myself, if SESW will refuse permission to any telecommunications company to erect a mast in Nork Reservoir.

To guard against the risk of this letter's going astray in your office, I am sending it recorded delivery (RT933864091 GB).

We were then in for a long wait. As on the last occasion when this part of the world was under threat of aerial bombardment, in the 1940s, we kept ourselves going with a little gentle humour at the expense of our tormentors.

Should we always refer to Lord MacLaurin of Knebworth by his full title and dignity? One of my respondents when I was canvassing had said that she was reminded of P. G. Wodehouse; and, although Lord MacLaurin of Knebworth is not in the higher reaches of Augustus Fink-Nottle and the like, I had already thought of the Earl of Emsworth and the Empress of Blandings. But Lord MacLaurin was not in the same class as that amiable, absent-minded, pig-loving peer.

P. G. Wodehouse could not help us; we were on our own.

Lord Megafone? Not quite: his answers to my letters were understated to the point of total inaudibility. Lord MacVodafone of Cloud Nine? That's nearer the mark: it catches his Olympian remoteness from the concerns of ordinary mortals. Lord...?

The outcome

Councillor Norman Harris kindly telephoned me on 4 May to say that SESW were withdrawing permission for the Vodafone mast to be built on their land at Nork Reservoir. Mary was in touch with me soon after to say that Phil Holder's decision on this matter was not unequivocal. She thought it would be helpful if a number of us wrote in to him to thank him for his decision; this would make it more difficult for him to renege. Her circular of 7 May with its compliments to Phil Holder, which I helped to distribute, is reproduced as Appendix Q.

I had a letter dated 11 May from Nick Greer saying that 'Sutton and East Surrey Water have confirmed that they do not wish to proceed with this site at this stage'. This letter was sent first class. I had a letter dated 17 May from Phil Holder saying that 'for a number of reasons we would prefer it if Vodafone did not use our Nork Reservoir site for a radio pole'.

By an extraordinary coincidence, this happy outcome became known on 4 May, two days before the local elections of 6 May, in which the Nork Residents' Association had a political interest. A leaflet was widely distributed on 5 May saying the following:

Nork Residents' Association

STOP PRESS...

NO MAST AT NORK RESERVOIR

We have just heard that the Association's protests since being informed of the proposed mast, together with those of local residents, have led to the Water Board withdrawing permission from Vodaphone for the erection of this structure on their site.

For 'Water Board' read 'Water Company' and for 'Vodaphone' read 'Vodafone'; otherwise this leaflet is acceptable as a partisan effort.

An item, 'No masts for Nork' appeared in *Nork Quarterly*, Summer 1999, page 17, over the byline of Councillor Norman Harris:

> Following talks with the Sutton & East Surrey Water Company, a Vodaphone mast on the Nork Reservoir at the rear of Lancaster Court, Eastgate and Green Curve has been turned down by Managing Director Mr. Phil Holder. Affected residents should have received a letter from him indicating his decision. I would like to take this opportunity of thanking Dr. Mary Saunders of Green Curve for all her help in persuading Mr. Holder that this was not a good site. Visiting the area with the Director finally did the trick, together with the volume of letters of objection from local residents.
>
> An application for another mast at Nork Community Centre was also rejected by the Council, as the Centre occupies Council-owned land.

Perhaps more interestingly, after SESW eventually withdrew permission for the mast (on 4 May), the *Banstead Herald* carried a report (on 9 June) explaining that Councillor Norman Harris had 'co-ordinated the people power protest from hundreds of people in the area'. This report was rather late in the day. The Banstead and District *Independent* had led with this story on 12 May, also mentioning Councillor Norman Harris but without imputing to him the role of coordinator. I might even have thought that I had been the coordinator, had not the *Banstead Herald* explained that this role had been played by Coordinator Norman Harris. I was physically in the front line of this battle, and my interest in the matter was known to Coordinator Harris throughout. I knew that he was in touch with Mary and SESW; but his coordinating activities eluded me entirely. He left me completely uncoordinated. His is indeed the art that conceals art, the coordination that conceals coordination.

7

OTHER SITES

Although this book is mostly about a successful campaign against a Vodafone mast on Sutton and East Surrey land at Nork Reservoir, other masts proposed or erected in the neighbourhood at around the same time throw a ray of light on the Nork Reservoir story and its implications:

- Nork Park: Vodafone mast on Reigate and Banstead Borough Council land;
- Ruxley Lane Ewell: BT Cellnet mast on privately owned land;
- Banstead Station: BT Cellnet mast in the former stationmaster's garden, on land now owned by Banstead Builders' Merchants (BBM).

Nork Park

Vodafone applied on 16 March (the day after Mary and I heard about the proposed Vodafone mast at Nork Reservoir) to erect a 15-metre mast within the curtilage of the Nork Community Centre, used by the Nork Community Association and others. There would be three directional antennae and two dish antennae on top. There would also be an equipment cabin of not more than 30 cubic metres. The purpose of development was 'in particular to provide improved coverage to Nork village'. I have lived in this neighbourhood almost all my life, and I still do not know where Nork village is. Nor, I suspect, do Vodafone; the use of this phrase provides a vivid illustration of Vodafone's insensitivity to local concerns when making their plans in a remote office in Berkshire.

Norman Harris, in a letter to me dated 16 April, said that the Vodafone Nork Park application was not a substitute for the Reservoir site but an addition.

The application was date-marked 22 March by Reigate and Banstead Planning Department. The land is owned by Reigate and Banstead Council and leased to the Community Association. The Council's status as landowner was confirmed by a check of the deeds. Thus the Council could refuse permission as landowners.

Peter North, of Reigate and Banstead's Legal and Estates Services section of the Resources Department, said in a letter of 9 April to Councillor Harris that the Planning Team considered the proposal to be 'dreadful'. So did I, but no more dreadful than the proposed mast at Nork Reservoir. The two would be very near different sets of residents and would be unacceptable to residents over wide areas with a substantial overlap.

If the Council officials (who make the decisions in these matters under delegated authority) were so much against the mast and the land was owned by the Council, that should have been the end of the matter. Councillor Harris was against the mast, as emerged later, and other Councillors may have been against it too. But this open-and-shut case was the only one known to me in which the Nork Residents' Association thought fit to be involved before the Council's determination. In a circular of 13 April, over his name and headed 'Please read urgently', A. I. Haward, in his capacity as Honorary Secretary of Nork Residents' Association, asked 'residents in the vicinity of Nork Community Centre' to send a very short note of objection by 15 April, 'quoting Vodafone 99P/0388, to Nigel Clifford, Director of Environmental Services (Attention Mr H. Watson, Development Control), Environmental Services Department, Reigate and Banstead Council'. 'You can, if you wish,' he said, 'have an effect on such decisions if you act now.'

This circular brings to mind the old conundrum about who does which, and with what, and to whom. If the Council's Legal and Estates Services had already decided on 9 April that Vodafone's Nork Park application was 'dreadful' and had so informed Councillor Norman Harris, who was sitting on the Council in the political interest of the Nork Residents' Association, why was it necessary for the Honorary Secretary of the Association on 13 April to issue an urgent appeal to residents in the vicinity of Nork Community Centre to write to the Environmental Services Department? Was the Environmental Services Department, whose ear the residents were exhorted to bend, not on speaking terms with Legal and Estates Services, whose ear was apparently already bent? If the Nork Residents Councillors were a cipher in these transactions, under the principle of delegated authority, was there nevertheless a risk that Councillors of other political persuasions from other wards would somehow get in on the act and override the wishes of the Residents' Association Councillors from Nork? Did the Residents' Association not trust the Residents' Association Councillors? Did the Councillors not trust the Legal and Estates Services section of the Resources Department? Did...? Not for the first time in this affair, the mind boggled.

Events moved with supersonic speed. In a letter dated 16 April 2000, Councillor Norman Harris informed me that 'his efforts had been successful, as per enclosed copy letter from Reigate and Banstead Borough Council to Vodafone'. (I take his word for this, although the 'enclosed' copy letter has not reached me yet.) He added: 'I understand that the Council had a great number of letters following the Residents' Association leaflet to residents in the immediate area, which assisted us in our efforts.' But who was 'us' and who was 'our'? The letter was headed 'Reigate and Banstead Borough Council: Nork Residents' Association'. Who were making 'efforts' and against whom were these 'efforts' directed? If the Residents' Association was not making efforts against its own Councillors, was it making efforts against the Council as a whole, including Councillors of other persuasions from other wards? Or was it making efforts against the Council's staff, who were once paid to do as they were told but had now, like the cuckoo, ejected the democratically elected Councillors from the nest that was rightfully theirs? Why were any 'efforts' or 'assistance' required at all? What on earth was going on?

I am grateful to Councillor Harris for documents about the Nork Park site. The evidence known to me indicates that he acted quickly and effectively in securing the desirable outcome of no Vodafone mast in Nork Park. But, if the residents and the Councillors were of one mind, and if the Council owned the land and could thus veto the mast, what puzzles me is why there should have been any call on Councillor Harris to display these qualities of leadership.

Ruxley Lane, Ewell

The BT Cellnet mast at Ruxley Lane, Ewell, went up shortly before Mary and I heard about the threat of a Vodafone mast at Nork Reservoir. According to the Epsom *Informer* of 11 March, Ainsley de Robillard had 'just seen a 15 metre Cellnet tower erected at the end of his garden in Ruxley Lane, Ewell'.

This mast had never been accepted by residents of the built-up area. Mr de Robillard, who had campaigned against the erection of the mast, continued his campaign after it had been erected. He attracted the attention of his MP, Sir Archibald Hamilton, and of Mohamed Fayed, the owner of Harrods, although I do not know that either of them succeeded in offering effective help. He also wrote to John Prescott, the Minister responsible for these masts; but some months later he had had no reply. I know the feeling.

Dr Rolf Bachen, who lives 50 metres from the mast, wrote to Tony Blair (Epsom, Banstead and Leatherhead *Informer*, 15 April 1999). I hope he got more sense out of the Prime Minister than I did. He said that the erection of masts constituted 'a bigger crisis than BSE' and noted that in New South Wales, Australia, masts were not allowed to be erected within 500 metres of schools, hospitals and homes because of fears about the possible health risks.

If Hamilton, Fayed, Prescott and Blair did not succeed in offering effective help, Mr de Robillard got more sense out of his Councillor, Mrs Jean Smith of the Independent Residents' Association, Epsom and Ewell, and more sense than I have ever got out of my Councillors. Mrs Smith announced in a letter to the Epsom *Informer* of 11 March that in response to pressure from her and others, 'in future it will be mandatory to display publicly any planning applications for these masts and to consult potentially affected residents. Moreover, the period for residents to object is to be extended from 28 days to 45 days.' Mrs Smith has also continued to campaign for the erected mast to be moved. An account of her activities, which she wrote for this book, is given in Appendix R. Some of her wording appeared in the Epsom and Leatherhead *Independent*, 18 November 1999.

BBM Banstead Station

I first heard about this proposed mast from a throwaway line in a letter of 31 March 1999 about Nork Reservoir from George Hinton, Chairman of Nork Residents' Association. He said, 'Another cellphone provider, Securicor, has recently stated an intent to erect a mast on the premises of Banstead Builders' Merchants at Banstead Station. Vodafone ought to be able to negotiate a sharing agreement to use this mast rather than erect another within 2–300 metres.' I did not like the idea of merely shifting the mast instead of getting it out of Nork altogether; but this depressing news was worth having in case there was any chance of stopping the mast at Banstead Station. Mr Haward's Residents' Association circular of 13 April said: 'There are already two proposals outstanding, one near Banstead station and one at Nork Reservoir on which we are negotiating', a form of words which does not make it clear whether the Association purported to be negotiating on one or both of these proposals. It soon became clear that there was and had been no negotiation on BBM Banstead Station.

In a letter of 20 April to Councillor Harris, I said:

The Securicor mast at BBM would be almost as near to these flats as the Vodafone mast at Nork Reservoir and would in some ways be worse, as the rays would be directly beamed at the balconies where we have for many years sat out in the summer. You have recently told me that your personal position is – no new masts or upgraded facilities in Nork. The BBM mast is in Nork and I was glad to see that you are opposing it (if that is indeed the meaning of 'two proposals outstanding, one near Banstead Station and one at Nork Reservoir on which we are negotiating'). If you would like me to leave the BBM negotiations to you, I should be grateful if you would give me an indication of what you are doing.

(In a letter of 16 April he had asked me 'not to get involved with this latest application' [Nork Park] 'as I would handle it'.) In a letter of 24 April he said: 'The Banstead Builders' Merchants site for Securicor was passed some time ago, and if you want to "have a go" yourself feel free to do so.'

An application had been submitted to Reigate and Banstead on 18 January 1999 by Cellular Design Services of Horsham, Sussex, for what was described as 'a 15-metre high monopole with antennae and ancillary equipment' at BBM, Banstead Station. Cellular Design was acting on behalf of Telecom Securicor Cellular Radio Ltd. The phrase '15 metre' requires interpretation. The road and entrance to Banstead Station are 39 steps above the level of the passenger platform, which in turn is the usual height above the railway track. The proposal was to build the mast 'on a piece of land raised up from the drive', which is at the level of the railway track. The mast would have a height of 15 metres above the 'piece of land raised up', which would compensate for the lower level of the drive (or railway track) and bring the base of the mast to the level of the road. Councillor Selby is recorded as having made no objections. The officials did not 'consider an application to be required, given the location and nature of the site' and recommended that 'prior approval was not required'. R. N. Clifford, Reigate and Banstead Director of Environmental Services, wrote to Cellular

Design in this sense on 16 February, 'acting in accordance with his delegated powers'.

Subsequently, Cellular Design had a change of plan and decided that it would be cheaper or otherwise preferable to site the mast at road level on land immediately behind BBM's offices (in the south west corner of the former station master's garden), the overall height of the mast remaining the same: the mast would not have to be based on raised land. This required a new application from Cellular Design, since a former application that had already been 'determined' could not be modified.

This provided an opportunity for the objections and protests that had been neglected in January. Appendix S reproduces my letter of 2 June to R. N. Clifford. It was copied to A. I. Haward, to Councillors Harris, Selby and Stead and to George Hinton, Chairman of Nork Residents' Association. I had a formal acknowledgement dated 8 June from Councillor Selby and a letter from A. I. Haward dated 14 June saying that my letter had been discussed by the Residents' Committee on 8 June, when Councillor Harris had been asked to comment on behalf of them all. No comments from Councillor Harris have reached me. I also had a form letter from R. N. Clifford, dated 14 June and addressed to me as Dear Sir/Madam, informing me that 'prior approval is not required... On the basis that this is an alternative to that submitted (in January). Therefore details of siting and appearance be approved.'

Banstead Station was following the same pattern as Nork Reservoir (except that the Councillors, officials and Residents' Association had made life even more difficult for the residents than before by quietly letting through an earlier and related application).

I had already written to BBM on 1 May offering to pay the fee that they would receive from Securicor. I believed Securicor to be the right name on the basis of information sent to me on 31 March by George Hinton, Chairman of the Nork Residents' Association. My letter to BBM is reproduced as Appendix T. It was sent recorded delivery; but I had no reply.

At Nork Reservoir, the operator was less friendly, or more unfriendly, than the landowner. At Banstead Station it proved to be the other way round, as I suspected it would. The next step was to get in touch with Securicor, which I did on 1 May. I wrote to the Chairman, Sir Neil Macfarlane, and had a reply from Nigel Griffiths, Director and Company Secretary, who was the politest commercial correspondent I had encountered so far (with little competition from some of the others). He explained that the mast concerned was a BT Cellnet one; Securicor had no masts of its own. Securicor was a 40 per cent owner of BT Cellnet. BT Cellnet was the generic name for the Cellnet group of companies and one of the subsidiaries within that group was Telecom Securicor Cellular Radio Ltd, which was the company which operated the cellular network in the United Kingdom. Earlier, there had been just the one cellnet company, called Telecom Securicor Cellular Radio Ltd. The Securicor name had remained with that company and would continue to do so because Securicor owned 40 per cent of the Cellnet group. I was grateful for this lucid exposition of a complicated subject. BT have since bought out the remaining 40 per cent holding of Securicor in BT Cellnet.

Correspondence with BT and BT Cellnet

Nicholas Eldred, Company Secretary of BT Cellnet, wrote to me on 7 June at the request of Nigel Griffiths. He had taken time to discover the exact factual situation. On occasions [*sic*] people did have different perspectives on the siting of antennae. BT Cellnet were following due process and proceeding properly. Mr Eldred hoped that the contents of his letter had reduced my concerns.

My reply of 14 June to Nicholas Eldred is reproduced as Appendix U. I pointed out that SESW had already withdrawn permission for the erection of a Vodafone mast at Nork Reservoir because of the scale of local protest and that the people who would have been adversely affected by the mast at Nork Reservoir were much the same as the people who would be adversely affected by a mast at Banstead Station. I urged him to get in touch with SESW and with Vodafone to hear their account of why the proposed mast at Nork Reservoir had been abandoned. I wrote on 19 August to point out that residents of Ruxley Lane, Ewell, were still trying to have the BT Cellnet mast moved: it was easier, cheaper and pleasanter not to erect a mast than to move it once it had been erected.

Nicholas Eldred is a maestro of the eloquent silence. I had heard nothing in response to my letter of 19 August and so I wrote again on 18 October reminding him that SESW had respected local opinion which was much the same local opinion as a BT Cellnet mast at BBM Banstead Station would defy. He wrote back on 9 December saying that 'there are occasions when people do have different perspectives on the siting of antennae. I cannot really say much more than this'.

I wrote to Sir Iain Vallance, chairman of BT, by express post on 14 December. I pointed out that I had had no answer to the substance of my letter of 14 June (see Appendix U). Our experience belied the claim of BT Cellnet that they 'take into account local sensibilities'; SESW took local sensibilities into account, but BT Cellnet appeared to ignore them entirely. I had urged Nicholas Eldred to ask SESW why they had withdrawn permission for the erection of a mast at Nork Reservoir; as far as I know, he never did so. I asked that the mast at BBM Banstead Station be put on hold until a solution could be found that was less damaging to all concerned. My letter was acknowledged by John Rutnam.

The substantive reply to my letter of 14 December came in a letter of 5 January 2000 from Nadia Bagwell, Customer Resolution Executive, Customer Resolution Team, BT Cellnet, Leeds. Her letter was sent second class and arrived on 8 January. She said:

> I was sorry to learn of your dissatisfaction with the siting of the BT Cellnet mast at Banstead Station. The siting of the mast has been carefully considered with all factors borne in mind. The chosen position, situated in a Builders' yard in a low railway cutting, ensures that there is minimal impact to the physical features and amenity of the area. The installed mast will be a slim line monopole model, which assists with integration into the surrounding

environment. In addition, we believe that the area is well screened.

I could hardly believe my luck. What Nadia Bagwell said would be entirely acceptable. A mast 'in a low railway cutting' was not something I would wish to oppose. But I feared that her letter made no contact with BT Cellnet's plans, which I knew more about than she did. I wrote to Sir Iain Vallance, BT Chairman, by express post on 9 January urging that the mast be resited precisely as Nadia Bagwell had indicated. My letter is reproduced as Appendix V.

Events now moved fast. Building work started on 11 January, apparently for the erection of a mast in a completely different position from where Nadia Bagwell had assured me it would be sited. I faxed Sir Iain Vallance on 12 January:

'Further to my letter of 9 January, building work started yesterday and continues today, in the upper yard of Banstead Builders Merchants, at road level. The work is apparently the installation of a telecommunication mast. The site is as in my letter of 9 January, not as in Nadia Bagwell's letter of 5 January, which you have.

Are you willing to honour Nadia Bagwell's assurance that the mast will be 'in a low railway cutting'? Or is honour in short supply at BT Head Office?

If you are willing to honour her assurance, it would be best to discontinue the work forthwith, with a view to resiting the mast in the location specified by Nadia Bagwell.'

I sent a second fax later on 12 January asking: 'Are you or are you not willing to stand by the assurance that Nadia Bagwell gave me on behalf of BT Cellnet?' My communications of 9 and 12 January were acknowledged by John Rutnam on 12 January: a reply would be sent as soon as possible.

I was in London on 13 January and work on the mast had apparently been discontinued. Someone from BT Cellnet rang Ann and said that I would have a reply within three working days. I was at home on 14 January; Jonathan Carey rang me from BT Cellnet and said that I would have a reply within three working days.

On this one occasion, BT/BT Cellnet were as good as their word. The mast went up between the morning of Friday 14 January and the evening of Monday 17 January. No other reply has reached us. This studied insult was their reply (and for the first time in this sorry saga it came within the promised three working days). A company needs a visceral contempt for its shareholders, customers and neighbours to play a practical joke like that.

I wrote to Sir Iain Vallance on 5 February recounting these events, urging that the mast be re-sited as Nadia Bagwell had indicated and asking whether there was anyone at BT or BT Cellnet who told the truth or kept his word. The paladin of truth and honour who replied to me on 14 February was the same Nadia Bagwell who had been as wrong as she could be about the only matter of substance that BT/BT Cellnet had ever deigned to address: 'Firstly, please accept my apologies for the delay in response. I have been waiting on reports from our Network Planning Division. I am now in a position to confirm that the BT Cellnet mast is situated in Banstead Builders Merchant yard. Whilst the majority of the Builders Merchant yard is in a low railway cutting, I *now* understand that the mast is situated in an area that is not [italics mine].' Yes, sunshine, but that's the whole point at issue. You may understand this only now; but I have understood it all along. The problem is that the only answer or assurance I have ever had from BT Cellnet (a) came from an underbriefed underling in a remote fastness in Leeds; (b) took seven months to arrive; (c) was plumb wrong; and (d) reached me only when BT Cellnet had already decided to do something utterly different. Given this background, it is not surprising that BT Cellnet show no sense of shame and make no attempt to apologise.

A new vision for business

Those who behave the worst are often the keenest to preach to others. It came as no surprise to find that BT were represented on the Committee of Inquiry: *A New Vision for Business* in the persons of Jan Walsh (member of the Steering Committee) and Bill Cockburn, Group Managing Director (signatory of the introductory statement).

The report was published in November 1999. I cannot do justice here to the plummy ripeness of its prose; but a few excerpts may help to give the flavour. 'Companies are increasingly aware of their responsibilities ... to the communities in which they are located' (page 7). Like the residents of Nork near BBM Banstead Station? 'The eight sponsor companies are committed to the principles of social, environmental and ethical responsibility that permeate the Inquiry's output' (page 7). It is regrettable that these principles did not permeate BT's conduct. 'Partnerships with communities have to be *an open book – no secrets, no surprises*' (page 19) (italics in original). Well, it was a surprise to me when BT's mast at BBM Banstead Station went up at road level when I had been assured that it would be sited in a low railway cutting and had been told that my letters to the Chairman pointing this out would be answered within three working days. '*Doing right* needs to be interpreted at two levels' (page 20). One level is enough for me. 'The deeper educational task is ... to develop a business paradigm that reflects what it is to be human' (page 21). Forget the business paradigm; just try a spot of human decency. 'Consumers should not be exposed to risks that they cannot evaluate in advance, or over which they have no control' (page 56). Nor should neighbours. Again, a business should be perceived as a 'neighbour of choice' by its community and not as a 'dangerous intruder' (page 116). And which, pray, is a telecommunication mast erected in the teeth of local opposition? 'A new taskforce under the leadership of Bill Cockburn of BT is now investigating *Impact on Society* and how business can measure and report on the negative and positive impact it has on society' (page 118). The present book reports on the negative impact BT has had on Nork. 'A far higher level of transparency ... will be basic for the majority of companies' (page 160). Including BT.

Institutional incompetence?

I would not accuse BT of institutional dishonesty, even though the only promise to me that they have ever kept was the promise to answer within three days about BBM Banstead Station and the answer was to erect the mast precisely where they had assured me it would not be erected. But institutional incompetence might be nearer the mark. This is illustrated by the anecdote of the missing phone book.

Appendix W tells the story of my endeavours, starting in May 1999, to obtain a second copy of a phone book to which I am entitled by virtue of the equipment I rent from BT. This has been a problem for years; but on all previous occasions I got my book in the end. In 1999 BT apparently thought that they had been letting me off too lightly and that it would be fun to make the assault course more challenging. A really imaginative refinement, a strong candidate for the cheek-of-Old-Nick wooden spoon, is their 'inability to access any BT telephone service details from the address you have given us'. During the last 30 and more years, BT and its predecessors have never had any difficulty in 'accessing my service details' when they wanted to send me a bill by post.

I still haven't had my phone book, after four requests and a year's delay. If BT can make such a pig's breakfast out of supplying a phone book, it is hardly surprising that they lack subtlety and finesse in responding to a more complex challenge like local opposition to a telecommunication mast. Some of the BT characters who replied to me about the phone book also replied to me about the mast, and some of the letters on the two subjects were identical.

Part of the problem is simply poor communications. Communications have long been the weak point of BT. There are times when I feel like sending them a team of carrier pigeons to speed everything up. My endeavours to get through to them about the telecommunication mast by letter and fax were not rewarded with success. Perhaps I should have had more luck on the telephone; but I doubt it. You know the problem: 'If you wish to listen to a complete performance of

Vivaldi's *Seasons*, press 1. If you wish to speak to a young girl who is polite and pleasantly spoken but doesn't know the first thing about anything, press 2. If you wish to speak to Beggarofski, our Customer Care Department, press 3. If you wish to speak to Uncle Tom Cobley, press 4 ... If you wish to speak to our Chairman, Sir Iain Vallance, press 105'.

The problem is not just left hand-right hand syndrome (in which the patient's left hand does not know what his right hand is doing) nor even arm-and-elbow syndrome (in which the patient suffers a pathological inability to distinguish his arm from his elbow or a clifftop site from a site in a low railway cutting). It is not just that BT's handling of local opposition to a telecommunication mast in Nork is what Rothbard once called a work of John Stuart Mill – 'a vast kitchen midden of diverse and contradictory positions'.[1] The problem goes deeper, as is shown by the comparison between BT and SESW. The problem is institutional.

A tale of two companies

When Sutton and East Surrey Water became aware of local opposition to the erection of a Vodafone mast on SESW land at Nork Reservoir, they eventually changed their minds. This alone indicates that they respect their tradition of public service and that they had (and have) procedures, through the agency of Phil Holder or otherwise, for assessing the options: is it or is it not worthwhile to go ahead with this mast in the teeth of local opposition?

It is not easy to interpret BT's short form-letters and long, cavernous silences; but my reading of the runes is that there was (and is) no one at BT with the responsibility for assessing local opposition to a mast and deciding whether or not the game is worth the candle. If there is local opposition to a mast, BT's policy is apparently either to ignore the opposition or to beat it down and drive the project through. BT works within government guidelines, which permit the operator to do pretty well

---

[1] Murray N. Rothbard: *Classical Economics* (Edward Elgar, 1995), page 277.

whatever he likes. BT's thinking is apparently untouched by recent work, such as that of the Centre for the Analysis of Risk and Regulation.[2]

For operators who simply wish to drive their projects through, my dealings with BT point a number of morals and teach a number of lessons, which I have codified in the following ten-point plan.

Ten points for the operators

1. Always telephone your correspondent and promise a reply within three working days. This confuses the enemy and buys a little time.
2. On no account reply within three working days. There is no need to reply at all.
3. It is all right to send acknowledgements and the like by first class post; but, if ever you see fit to send a substantive reply, make sure it goes second class. This costs the enemy another day or two.
4. Intone a mantra. Few can surpass Nicholas Eldred's all-purpose put-down: *people have different perspectives on the siting of antennae: I cannot really say much more than this.*
5. Take seven months or more to send the enemy your first substantive reply. With any luck the mast will be up by then.
6. On no account address the matters of concern raised in correspondence by the enemy. (For example, why did SESW concede to local opposition?)
7. If there is anyone in your company who understands what is going on, on no account let him correspond with the enemy. Route your correspondence through people hundreds of miles away, who have never visited the site and fail to master their briefing on the only matter of substance they address.

---

[2]*The Launch: Risk and Regulation*, London School of Economics, December 1999.

8 If your spokesman inadvertently gives the enemy precisely the assurance he has been seeking, on no account honour that assurance.
9 If the enemy protests that your word is worthless and that nothing you say can be trusted, on no account apologise. Just carry on as before.
10 If possible, have your Chairman appointed as President of that citadel of political correctness, the Confederation of British Industry (CBI). Perhaps your Chairman and the CBI deserve each other. There your Chairman will have ample opportunity to lecture *Untermenschen* (like shareholders, customers and neighbours) on how they should comport themselves.

The operators and the politicians

A large part of the problem is the recent culture of non-communication which is now engulfing civilised discourse. If you want the Customer Care Department, you get Vivaldi's *Seasons*. If you want BT on the siting of masts, you get Nadia Bagwell of the Customer Resolution Executive (and what on earth is *that*?). If you want the Conservative Party on a reassessment of planning law, you get Ian Philps. If you want the snorkelling John Prescott, you get nothing at all.

BT is at the forefront of this culture of non-communication and non-consideration; but the real fault lies with the politicians who got us into this mess in the first place with their primary and secondary legislation on the siting of masts. Ah well, what can you expect? Ninety-nine per cent of politicians give the others a bad name.

No masts for Nork

The story of the mast at BBM Banstead station makes its own commentary on the activities of the Nork Residents' Association and its Nork Ward Councillors. I first heard about the BBM mast in a letter of 31 March 1999 from George Hinton, Association

Chairman, to whom I had written about Nork Reservoir. The Council officials, as usual, wanted to rubber-stamp the application and keep the residents in the dark. But where was the Residents' Association? Where was the Coordinator? Councillor Selby raised no objections to the application in January. On 24 April, Norman Harris said that I should feel free to 'have a go' at the Banstead Station mast; but my ability to do so had been gravely compromised by the inactivity of Councillors and Association in January. They were apparently no more active when the application was resubmitted in May. I have no evidence that any of them did anything effective to oppose the mast. I had no substantive answer from Councillors or Association to my letter of 2 June to R. N. Clifford (see Appendix S).

The headline 'No masts for Nork' in an article with the byline of Councillor Harris (*Nork Quarterly*, Summer 1999, page 17) is inaccurate and misleading. I recognise that Councillor Harris may not have been responsible for this headline; but someone was responsible. Banstead Station is within the boundary of Nork; and, at the time of writing and publishing this article in *Nork Quarterly*, a proposal to erect a mast there, which the Association and its Councillors had not lifted a finger to prevent, had been outstanding for months and still was so.

Neither at Nork Reservoir nor at Banstead Station did the Councillors or Nork Residents' Association initiate opposition to the proposed mast, although they were not averse to claiming credit for a satisfactory outcome at Nork Reservoir. The difference between the sites is that the Association and the Councillors sold the pass at Banstead Station months before the matter became known to residents. That made it more difficult for residents to mount the kind of campaign they mounted at Nork Reservoir, when they learned of the proposed intrusion in the nick of time. According to the *Independent* of 23 June 1999, Norman Harris had 'successfully fought and won two battles against masts being erected in his Ward'; and it is regrettable that Conquistador Harris was so laid back about the mast at Banstead Station that he merely told a freelance private soldier to 'feel free to have a go'.

8

HOW TO FIGHT BACK

What do you do if someone proposes to erect a mast near your home or business premises?

The first step is to find out who is the landowner on whose land the mast would be erected. If he is an unrelated third party over whom you have no direct influence, you may be in for a fight; most of this chapter discusses this situation. But if he is a related party, the problem may be more easily manageable.

If a telecommunication company ('Spidernet') tries to suborn a local golf club or rugby club or tennis club, Spidernet may be seen off in short order by officers' action or a members' revolt; there are recent precedents for these within a few miles of here. If the fly that Spidernet is seeking to entrap is a church, the problem may be more difficult: many churches are hard up through no fault of their own, some desperately so. There is then the ethical dilemma of a Faustian pact with Lord Mephistopheles: at what price and for what purpose do you sell your soul? If Spidernet's target is a school, there is a wide range of possibilities, depending on the status of the school and the influence of parents and others in the process of taking decisions.

Even Reigate and Banstead Borough Council succeeded in saying no to a Vodafone mast on their land in Nork Park. Even the National Trust supported a Members' Resolution (for the AGM on 6 November 1999) arguing that 'the National Trust should have a presumption against the development of mobile telecommunication masts on its land'. (Resolution in the name of Dr Sarah Jones of High Wycombe.) Clubs may be more difficult, because there may be an element of the membership in favour of a Faustian pact. Churches and schools may be more difficult again because the financial needs may be more pressing and the decision-making process more complex. But the difficulties are in another league when neighbours are at risk from a mast operated by one unrelated third party on land owned by another. This is the topic of the rest of this chapter.

Legal and planning activities

If a telecommunication company wishes to erect a mast on nearby land owned by a third party, it is advisable or even indispensable to fight initially on grounds of planning law. This is what we did; and we were fortunate to have the help of John, who is a professional in this area. The purpose is not primarily to persuade the local officials to whom submissions on this subject are nominally addressed. The officials' aim is to protect their own backs, which the legislation of 1983–1995 makes it easy for them to do. However much at fault they are, they have little or nothing to fear. Admittedly, if they side with the residents, they may have a long battle with the telecommunication operator; but if they side with the operator, the residents are unlikely to cause them trouble. The residents, after all, are only the poor numbskulls who pay their salaries; they do not have virtually bottomless pockets like the operators and the officials (the latter funded out of taxation by the residents themselves). The purpose of fighting on grounds of planning law is to establish credibility with the real players, the landowners and the operators.

Legal action is not an attractive option for residents. The law was drafted to do them down, and their opponents have virtually unlimited financial resources.

Environmental bodies

Residents who are hoping for help from environmental bodies would be well advised to think again. The Green movement has more important things to do than to help people who fear that their lives may be ruined by telecommunication masts.

Friends of the Earth (England) are not active on the subject of telecommunication masts. Friends of the Earth (Scotland) are, and Graeme MacAllister has appeared before a Parliamentary committee in London; but they cannot be expected to interest themselves in problems in Surrey that are ignored by their sister body in England.

The Council for the Protection of Rural England (CPRE) have a campaign briefing entitled 'Telecommunication Development' (November 1998). It is 34 pages of A4 and is the best such document I have seen. It contains a policy review (page 9) to which I revert in Chapter 9. It contains much useful background information on law and practice, not least Appendices 5 and 6 on recent telecommunication decisions, classified as refusals and objections overruled. Appendix 8 gives 'Ten Campaign Tips', reproduced here as Appendix X.

We had followed most of the CPRE ten tips (although their campaign briefing came into my hands after our own campaign was over). There may well be situations in which the CPRE campaign briefing is a master plan for victory. I do not believe that ours was one of them. If we had followed all their advice to the letter, we should still not have won. For us, their advice was a prescription for losing with dignity.

Our problem was simply stated, though less easily resolved. We had to persuade the landowner, or the operator, or both that their lives would be happier and more agreeable if the mast did not go up than if it did.

The landowner (SESW) and all the telecommunication companies are themselves of course environmentally aware, concerned, considerate, compassionate, caring; as John Fooks said to Sir Archibald Hamilton, 'I appreciate the concerns of our neighbours and we do make every effort to be a good neighbour at all our sites and we are mindful of environmental issues'. But fine words butter no parsnips. What good were these protestations of virtue to us in our hour of need? There is a short, sharp expression...

Earlier chapters have discussed the substance of our campaign. I conclude the present chapter with my own set of ten campaign tips, which are unlikely to be confused with those of the CPRE.

Campaigning

1 *Two stages*   Do your best on the legal and planning side; but recognise from the start that you are likely to fail because you are stitched up by the legislation of 1983–1995. Be prepared for Stage 2, a campaign addressed to the landowner and/or the operator.
2 *Target*   Pick as your primary target a landowner or operator with a genuine sense of civic concern and public responsibility. If a company with a hide as thick as Vodafone's or BT's is dealing with a small local landowner equally impervious to public opinion, you are probably lost. But if there is a chink in the armour of self-interest and self-satisfaction, exploit it to the full. Always go for the Chairman: why accept less when you can have the grand Panjandrum himself for the same price? If the Chairman is a prominent public figure, you may be able to mount an Operation Mickeytake.
3 *Circulars and petitions*   Send round a circular before collecting signatures, so as to reduce the time required for explanations and to increase the likelihood of a friendly reception. Engage helpers for the legwork: do not try to do everything yourself.
4 *Petitions and letters*   Letters carry more weight than petitions: some people are perceived as being willing to sign anything to get a caller off their doorstep. Do not circulate a form letter: letters should be individually drafted, however short.

5 *Recorded and registered post*   Send all important documents by recorded delivery or what used to be registered post and is now Royal Mail special delivery, so that your correspondents cannot deny having received what you sent. Keep a copy of all important documents sent through the post.

6 *Division of roles*   It may be helpful to have someone in the foreground for discussions and negotiations and someone in the background putting pressure on the landowner and/or operator. Guard against spokesmen selling the pass.

7 *Have ploys in reserve*   Be prepared to continue the campaign if landowner and operator both turn you down. Do not protest or make a nuisance of yourself at company AGMs. This is unlikely to be effective and is thus a waste of your time: it is too easy for the Chairman to handle the situation. Instead, check your investments and get your friends to do the same. If you have any shares in the landowner or operator, write in to complain; you will not get very far, but your letter will at least be an irritant for the company concerned. More to the point, if you have any investment trusts or unit trusts (or other collective investment vehicles such as Personal Equity Plans), check whether they are invested in the offending companies. If you have thrown away the last report from the IT or UT that gave this information, ring them up and ask for another copy. If they are invested in either of the offending companies, write to the Secretary of the IT or UT and ask them to reduce their holding because the company has behaved so badly. (Do not use the words 'ethical' or 'unethical', or they will probably just say that they are not an ethical trust; see 8, below.) Financial houses are often inefficient but seldom impolite. They will probably reply. (If they do not, send a copy of your letter after a week or two by recorded delivery.) They are unlikely to do as you say (not least because they need the offending companies

more than the latter need them); but this is not a comfortable background for even the largest company. Consider sending a copy of your letter to the offending company, particularly if the response from the finance house is this side of a total rejection. Substantial holdings in the telecommunication industry are considered obligatory by many finance houses; but this has its compensations for your campaign: most funds are likely to hold the major operators. The Association of Unit Trusts and Investment Funds (65 Kingsway, London, WC2B 6TD; 020 7831 0898) will send you free of charge 'The Directory: A comprehensive list from which to choose the funds that meet your needs' and 'The Managers: A comprehensive list of the members of the Association of Unit Trusts and Investment Funds'. You and your friends can ring the managers and ask for details of their funds (not cash, fixed interest or foreign). Identify the funds that hold the offending companies. Write to them saying that you had been considering investing in the ABC fund; but you have decided not to because of their holding in the XYZ company. You and your friends should not use the same form of words in writing to the same fund; but it is perfectly acceptable for the same individual to use the same form of words in writing to different funds, and this helps to reduce expense of time and typing costs. Similar principles apply to the Association of Investment Trust Companies (Durrant House, 8–13 Chiswell Street, London, EC1Y 4YY; 020 7282 5555), who will send you free of charge their 'Guide to Investment Trust Companies' and an issue of their 'Monthly Information Service'.

8 *Ethical trusts* Ethical trusts are a more difficult proposition. The problem is that 'dark-green' funds accept or reject whole industries or areas of corporate activity on ethical grounds and then within the accepted industries select individual firms on com-

mercial grounds. *Money and Ethics*, 1998 edition, is published by the Ethical Investment Research Service (EIRIS; 80–84 Bondway, London, SW8 1SF; 020 7840 5700). It lists 18 industries that 'funds avoid investing in'; the selection is a matter of opinion, since some of the industries they reject seem to me more ethical than some they accept. Telecommunications and mobile phones are not among the rejects. There is a section in *Money and Ethics* on health and safety breaches; but the criterion for disapproval is that a company has been prosecuted by the Health and Safety Executive. When you have identified the landowner and his line of activity, it may be worth checking *Money and Ethics* in case it suggests reasons for writing to any or all of the 32 ethical funds. In recent years, there has also been a growth of 'light-green' funds which make ethical choices within industries and not merely between them. For present purposes, 'light-green' funds may be a more promising area to investigate than 'dark-green'. A free guide to ethical investing with a lighter shade of green is available from financial advisers Holden Meehan on 0800 731 4508. Another contact is financial advisers Ethical Investors Group (020 7734 6471). These two firms advise investors; they do not manage funds. Both make ethical choices within industries and not merely between them. Lee Coates of Ethical Investors Group told me that he had philosophical problems with excluding whole industries (with perhaps one or two exceptions; he also said that he dislikes all the various 'green' labels as simplistic and misleading and prefers to consider what a particular firm is doing). For the purposes of the present book, the exclusion of whole industries is unhelpful, whereas the exclusion of particular firms may be useful.

9 *Look after yourself* You may find the campaign strenuous and stressful. Ann and I did. We made a number of out-of-character mistakes, putting on the

wrong clothes, cooking the wrong foods, taking the wrong turnings. One night I dreamt that I looked out of the window and saw a team of men in our garden, slashing and burning. So look after yourself. If canvassing might be an ordeal, dress the part. With an old-fashioned walking stick and a hat inherited from my father, I cultivated a mildly eccentric appearance intended to reassure householders that my purpose was not to steal their silver, rape their daughters or sell them double glazing. In the event, I was well received almost everywhere. When engaged in the legwork, do not go too fast; slow down from time to time. If you usually wear a jacket at work, take it off and turn up the heat to compensate. If you are a regular smoker or drinker, on no account cut down. If anything increase the dose, but not by much. Don't take my word for it. Although I am a doctor, I have no medical background. Consult your medical adviser. Better still, use your common sense.

10 *Press for a change in the law* The present book is my own contribution to this cause. Changing the law is the subject of the next chapter.

9

CHANGING THE LAW

The present statute law governing the erection of telecommunication masts should be changed. It came in unnoticed by the press, the public and even the politicians who allowed it to go through. It is based on the assumption that the interests of telecommunication companies are all-important and that the opinions of the masts' neighbours do not count. Telecommunication companies are within their rights in ignoring the interests of residents, schools, hospitals and other neighbours. They ought not to be able to do so.

The government is not to be trusted on questions of health. Its first priority is to seek political advantage. Its second priority is to save money. The health of the public comes further down the list. Beef on the bone was banned, although the risk of harm is negligible or zero. Telecommunication masts are permitted in built-up areas although a substantial element of scientific opinion regards them as a health hazard, at least in the longer term. If the government finds it has made a mistake, its response is a cover-up, as in the organo-phosphorus sheep-dip scandal, publicised by the Countess of Mar in the House of Lords and by Christopher Booker in his Notebook articles in the *Sunday Telegraph*.

Nor is the government to be trusted on questions of policy. It is the government and Parliament that have created the present mess and they are unlikely of their own volition to put matters right. Pressure will be required to secure change of any kind, and an element of independent judgement will be required to ensure that the changes are a real improvement.[1]

It is beyond the scope of this book to propose a detailed programme of reform; but the present chapter starts with an abbreviated account of the programme published by the Council for the Protection of Rural England in November 1998 (*A Campaign Briefing: Telecoms Development*, page 9) and goes on to make a number of additional suggestions.

Council for the Protection of Rural England

The CPRE believes that the planning approach to telecommunications development at the national and local level should be revised as follows:

- Permitted development rights should be removed for all but the smallest telecommunications developments.
- Proposals subject to prior approval (if permitted development rights are retained) should be subject to an eight-week consultation period and should be publicised in the same fashion as planning applications.
- The Government's planning policy guidance should be revised to remove the bias in favour of the telecommunications industry.

---

[1] As I was putting this book into final form, I received the first word of sympathy that I had had from anyone in a position of authority. Andrew Lansley, MP, Shadow Minister for the Cabinet Office, writing in a private capacity on 16 February 2000, said: 'I am interested in telecoms masts, not least in a constituency capacity. The need for a roll-out across the country was the basis for the General Development Order. That time has, in my view, passed. I think we could now move to a conventional planning regime based on need, balanced against intrusion and proximity limits regarding microwave radiation emissions, the effects of which are by no means proven to be harmful, but are the subject of ongoing research.' On 1 March the Conservative Media Unit published a seven-point plan to stop 'monster masts' (generally masts over 15 metres). Tessa Jowell, the Health Minister, set up an expert committee in April 1999 under Sir William Stewart; it was reported (*Daily Express*, 28 February) that this committee would recommend curbs on masts. This Independent Expert Group on Mobile Phones reported in the first half of 2000: its report recommended additional curbs on the siting of masts and gave additional credence to a number of the health concerns mentioned in the present book.

- Operators should be obliged to consult the local planning authority on their plans for the whole of their network so that it may be organised so as to minimise environmental impact.
- New masts should only be considered as a last resort where the operator can demonstrate that there is no other way of providing the required component of the network.
- In cases of disagreement over the technical constraints concerning a network or individual mast the operator, at the request of the Local Authority, should be obliged to commission a report from an independent technical expert.
- The terms of the operator licences granted by the Department of Trade and Industry should be amended to reflect the changes in planning policy and control which are outlined above.

Other bodies as well as CPRE and Friends of the Earth (Scotland) are working to make the law less hostile to residents and other neighbours of masts. The Local Government Association (Local Government House, Smith Square, London, SW1P 3HZ) have published *LGA Response to Draft Advice to Local Planning Authorities on Land-use Planning and Development Giving Rise to Electromagnetic Fields* (April 1999). Powerwatch (2 Tower Road, Sutton, Ely, Cambs., CB6 2QA) have published *Cellular Phone Base – Station and Masts*.

Other proposals

Although early Government action on some elements of the problem is desirable and possible, the problem as a whole is so contentious and complex, and the Government is so committed to its present policies, however mistaken, that the best solution is unlikely to be approximated without an element of independent judgement. An independent Committee of Inquiry, with a brief to consider submissions from all quarters, could examine possible solutions that have so far been excluded from consideration through the one-sidedness of the law. The Government have recently set up a Committee with a wide remit on the still more contentious subject of foxhunting.

One perspective that should not be rejected is that masts as we know them may be overtaken by events. The National Trust says: 'In view of the rapid development of telecommunications technology, it is likely that the need for telecommunication masts will be ephemeral.' (Response to Members' Resolution submitted by Dr Sarah Jones, Agenda Item 5 Resolution D, Annual General Meeting, 6 November 1999.) If this assessment of the future is well founded, the implication is that few of these masts should be erected and that effort and expense should be redirected towards alternative technologies. For this and other reasons, telecommunication companies should not be under an obligation to provide a minimum standard of coverage [see Appendix A (3) of the present book].

Increased pressure on operators to make their masts compatible and share them with each other would at least reduce the number of masts even if it did not reduce the quantity of their emissions.

I have been in trouble with one or two libertarian friends on the ground that I was arguing in this book for an extension of state control over private industry. I do not see the matter like that. Long before telecommunication masts were invented, there were restrictions on a landowner's use of the space above his land. Restrictions on building under the English legal principle of ancient lights are an example: windows that had been used without interruption for at least 20 years created a right to prevent the owner of adjoining land from obstructing the light received through these openings. This is a principle of common and civil law, not of criminal or statute law. The owner of adjoining land was prevented from casting a shadow. In the opinion of their critics, telecommunication masts send out, not darkness, but disease and death.

There is scope for market-based and property-based solutions to the problem. In particular, those affected could be allowed the opportunity to buy out the operator or the landowner or both. Residents would then have a chance to vote with their wallets. My offers to pay the telecommunication company's fee were ignored by SESW and by BBM. This is an example of market failure caused by ill-drafted legislation.[2]

In a discussion of land-use planning going well beyond the siting of telecommunication masts, John Corkindale has argued in favour of 'structuring the law so as to minimise the impediments to private agreements'.[3] In this broader context, Corkindale recommends a system of impact fees, such as are employed in many land-use planning jurisdictions in North America and elsewhere; the replacement of designated areas by tradeable development rights; and the use of auctions and tendering procedures for planning permission.

The planning process is also susceptible of being reformed politically. John Redwood has proposed that planning should be devolved to the lowest level – the parish – and with no appeal. Matt Ridley has commented: 'Developers would have to appeal to locals instead of relying on civil servants to impose their wishes for them... The bureaucratic superstructure of the planning system, with its Soviet belief in knowing what is best for people, would vanish, together with the parasitic pressure groups that feed on it and swap employees with it'.[4]

Within the present planning system, a significant minimum distance might be imposed between masts and their victims. Dr Bachen has noted that in New South Wales masts are not allowed to be erected within 500 metres of schools, hospitals and houses because of fears about the possible health risks. Councillor Smith is also campaigning for a minimum distance (see Appendix R).

The burden of proof could also be reversed. Councillor Smith

---

[2]Property-rights approaches to planning are discussed in *Reforming Land-Use Planning* (Institute of Economic Affairs Studies on the Environment No.12, 1999).
[3]'*Land development in the United Kingdom: private property rights and public policy objectives*', Environment and Planning A, 1999, page 2053. This is what Cooter and Ulen (*Law and Economics*, HarperCollins, 1998) have called the 'Normative Coase Theory' on the basis of the seminal article by R. H. Coase, The problem of social cost (*Journal of Law and Economics*, 3 (1), pages 1–44, 1960).
[4]The *Daily Telegraph*, 2 November 1999. Redwood, *The Death of Britain?* (Macmillan, 1999, page 14).

has noted that in England masts are considered safe until proved dangerous, whereas in the USA and New Zealand the reverse applies and they are deemed harmful until proved safe.

The CPRE's idea of an independent technical expert could be extended to an independent financial arbitrator. At present, either the mast goes up and the residents are uncompensated or the mast does not go up and the landlord is uncompensated. Everything is decided by confrontation and forms of political pressure. If money passed to or from the residents, there could be two partially satisfied parties rather than one satisfied and one totally dissatisfied.

Another extension of the idea of an independent arbitrator is that permission for masts should be given for a limited period only. In other legislative contexts, this kind of time limit is often known as a 'sunset clause'. Contentious activities should not be licensed once and for all: the question should be reconsidered after a stated term. This has a number of advantages. The victims are not condemned to a life sentence but to a limited number of years. Changing circumstances can be brought into account. And the telecommunication companies may not be willing to go ahead on this basis. An independent arbitrator should have an important role in such a reassessment; the company would have an interest in saying that the mast is as important as ever it was.

When the balance of the argument indicates that a mast is technologically redundant, the company should be obliged to take it away and make good, and not leave it disfiguring the landscape.

In endeavouring to reform the system you will need allies. The politicians will ignore you if they can. The Radio 4 *You and Yours* programme on 16 and 17 November 1999 said that audience response had proved the existence of many hundreds of local anti-mast groups. The local press (including free sheets) may well name groups near you or be willing to answer questions on the subject. Other groups may be willing to share their experience with you or cooperate in matters such as obtaining publicity. Countrywide, cooperation between groups would be a tough assignment to organise; but it may be the only way to attract the politicians' attention. Remember the Countryside Alliance, which at least delayed, and may have removed, the threat of a ban on foxhunting. The Internet could be a way of getting in touch with like-minded activists elsewhere in the country (code words: masts, mobiles, health hazards, cancerous rays, etc.). If you are a member of Friends of the Earth (England), press them to join in the good work being done on masts by Friends of the Earth (Scotland). If you are a member of a voluntary body that owns land, alert them to the problem and ask for a commitment not to allow the siting of masts on their land, as Dr Sarah Jones of Wycombe did with the National Trust. Consider the possibility of cooperating with bodies addressing separate but related problems: for example, planning blight has been a problem for a generation or so, and planning blight has much in common with mast blight.

Finally, be imaginative in your search for allies. Public support for anything depends largely on empathy and identification. Look for people with recognisably similar problems to yours. My sympathy for Survival (International) has been heightened by my encounter with Vodafone. The problems of Survival's tribal peoples were much the same as mine with Vodafone: a bunch of alien intruders ruining my peaceful way of life by threatening my health and destroying the value of my habitat. At the simplest level, members of genuinely oppressed minorities (I do *not* mean minorities favoured by the politically correct, such as homosexuals, British ethnics or the Irish Republican Army) may serve common interests by banding together. A year or two ago, I attended a meeting where a speaker for the independence of East Timor was followed by speakers for the independence of Tibet. At the time of writing, East Timor is on the road to independence, at the cost of a bloody struggle that has almost destroyed the country. Hardly any of the internationally Good and Great lifted a finger to help East Timor in its hour of need. East Timor's success was achieved by persistence and determination, internally and externally, against an Indonesian Government that eventually had more important preoccupations. Tibet has more substantial and determined opponents. Victims of masts are somewhere between East Timor and Tibet. They are unlikely to win in a year or two, even after a hard struggle. But they have some hope of winning before their way of life has been destroyed by hostile invaders. And Tibet has something to teach us about outreach to potential sympathisers in the most unpropitious circumstances: when I was writing this chapter, I received a mailing from the Free Tibet Campaign including a flyer for Save the Rhino International.[5] While I was under threat from Vodafone, I felt as endangered as any rhino. Similarly, Survival's campaign for the Innu Indians of Northern Canada is entitled 'Canada's Tibet – The Killing of the Innu'. 'Tibet' is now an internationally-known and immediately-recognisable symbol of cultural and physical genocide. Tibetans and their friends have shown the potential for enrolling allies. Their example needs to be followed by opponents of masts.

---

[5] Save the Rhino International is at Winchester Wharf, Clink Street, London, SE1 9DG, telephone: 020 7357 7474.
Survival (International) is at 11–15 Emerald Street, London, WC1N 3QL, telephone: 020 7242 1441.
The Free Tibet Campaign is at 1 Rosoman Place, London, EC1R 0JY, telephone: 020 7833 9958.

10

OUTRAGE!

Why is this fellow making such a fuss? you may ask. A mast is just a mast. There are many worse things happening all over the world. Quite apart from earthquakes and other natural disasters, there are wars and civil wars and genocides: Tibet, Sudan, Chechnya. Even at home, there are the horrors chronicled, for example, by Christopher Booker in his Notebook in the *Sunday Telegraph* and by John McLean in his book *Tyranny of the Law: How the Law is Taking away our Liberties*.[1]

Well said. Yes, there are many worse off than I, who was merely at risk of having my health shattered and my property rendered all but unsaleable by Vodafone. One ought to keep these things in proportion.

That said, a fight against what is wrong and unacceptable may still be worth fighting, even if it is a small fight, and especially if it is winnable. In addition, I was goaded into action by the indifference or contempt with which I was treated by Council staff, Councillors, Residents' Association, politicians... We were *contra mundum*, as they say in *Brideshead Revisited*: against the world. The problem is not so much the telecommunication companies, as the politicians and civil servants who have given these companies the power to walk all over us.

This book has a message for politicians and others: things do

---
[1] Winter Productions Limited, Jersey, 1999.

not have to be as bad as this, there are better ways. It also carries a message of good cheer for those (like most of those I canvassed) who feel a sense of Outrage! against the politicians and others who got them into this mess and always have something more important to do than get them out of it.

This message of good cheer and goodwill for those who may be under threat from Vodafone, BT or any other telecommunication company also exists in army dog-Latin. There are several versions; but this is the most canonical: *non ab illegitimis carborundum* – don't let the bastards grind you down.

Postscript

As I was checking the proofs of this book, I heard of the success of residents of Ruden Way and nearby roads, under the leadership of Clare Mann, in seeing off a proposal to erect a One2One mast on an alley beween Ruden Way and Epsom Downs railway station, a little over a mile away from Nork Reservoir. Their campaign differed from ours, which may have helped theirs. First, they were informed in time by Reigate and Banstead Borough Council. Second, they had much of 42 days to campaign, as compared with our 12 or less. Third, they were thus able to amass much more support (about 1000 objections). Fourth, their sympathetic ear was not that of the landowner (Railtrack, which was surprising, given Railtrack's difficulties at the time) but of the operator (One2One). However, they secured this sympathy by dint of looking for alternative sites, which we did not.

APPENDIX A

The legislative background

The relevant legislation is listed in footnote 1 on page 5. The following brief description of its effects is abstracted from *A Campaign Briefing: Telecoms Development* of November 1998 (CPRE, November, paragraphs 1, 2, 4, 5) and *Briefing: Blot on the Horizon or Health Threat?* [Friends of the Earth (Scotland), January 1999: paragraphs 3, 6].

1   Operators enjoy extensive permitted development rights (PDRs) which remove the requirement to submit a full Planning Application for proposed masts not exceeding 15 metres. An operator has to notify the local planning authority of its proposal and provide information on the application. The local Planning Authority has only 28 days in which to determine whether its prior approval for the siting and appearance of the proposed development is required and in which to make a determination. The 28 days begin from the time when full information on the application is received. There are no statutory requirements for any publicity or consultation. Only in circumstances where a Local Authority can show that 'the exercise of a permitted development right can have a serious impact on amenity' can they issue an Article 4 direction – which withdraws PDRs. (This means that

a developer then has to apply for planning permission.) In the case of telecommunication masts, however, the Secretary of State's prior approval is required for such a direction and there may be the risk of compensation. Although a Local Authority may not prevent the development in principle, they can require changes to the siting and appearance to protect amenity. If a Local Authority does refuse prior approval details, the developer has a right of appeal.

2 Under a separate procedure under the Telecommunications Act 1984 the operator's licence requires them to notify the local Planning Authority of the whole of the proposed local network for the area at the same time as the first proposal is submitted. The *Telecommunications Prior Approval Procedures (Code of Best Practice)* recommends that this is done before any determination or planning application is made (para. 2.1, i) and that the details of the existing network are also provided. Currently, a Local Authority has 28 days to raise any concerns and 40 days for concerns relating to certain nationally designated areas (for example, an Area of Outstanding Natural Beauty).

3 Network operators are also accorded fairly strong legal powers through the Telecommunications Act 1984. Under Schedule II of the Act, the mobile phone companies were awarded licences to operate networks as telecommunications code operators and as such were required to provide network coverage to 90 per cent of the country by 31 December 1999. If this target was not achieved, the operator's licence could be revoked. In pursuance of their aim to provide network coverage they were also given rights similar to those of compulsory purchase orders. If a landowner rejects their approach to erect a transmitter on his or her property then a code operator can apply to the courts to allow them to dispense with consent for that site and assess the financial recompense to be awarded to the landowner.

4   Although a planning application must be submitted for masts over 15 metres, Government policy in Planning Policy Guidance (PPG) note 8 takes a very positive view of the growth of the telecommunications industry. The guidance states, in paragraph 6, that the need for such services should not be questioned, and in paragraph 26 that 'applications should not be refused on the basis of policies which take insufficient account of the growth ... of telecommunications'.

5   Paragraph 29 of the guidance suggests that the special needs of apparatus, for example technical constraints, may outweigh the adverse effects such as the visual impact of new masts. This clearly suggests that the needs of the telecommunications industry may sometimes be placed higher than the need to protect even the most sensitive of landscapes from intrusive development. Established national policies, such as those concerning Areas of Outstanding Natural Beauty seem to carry less additional weight in relation to these forms of development.

6   There are few options available to you if you wish to oppose the siting of a base station transmitter or challenge the location of an existing transmitter. The planning system, as it stands, does not offer a satisfactory means of opposition particularly if your concerns are on health grounds, as it is all too easy for a Planning Authority to refer to current National Radiological Protection Board guidelines and reject your concerns.

APPENDIX B

John Popham and the Council

This appendix contains extracts from correspondence between John Popham and Reigate and Banstead Council officials in Spring 1999, together with related material.

1 J. P. to R. N. Clifford, 22 March 1999

My concern ... is to draw to your attention the difficulty in which my clients find themselves, through no fault of their own, by your Council's failure to follow the Secretary of State's advice and 'encourage publicity' relating to this non-statutory application. As you will be aware, publicity should have included the setting of an adequate publicly stated timescale by which a response should be made (see Circular 9/95, Appendix E, para 5).

A consequence of your failure to publicise this application for prior approval is that on receipt of my clients' objection your authority will have very limited time in which to give proper consideration to the objections which you have received and investigate the points which have been raised – in particular those relating to the need to use the application site.

Recent High Court decisions have demonstrated that public concern, in the form of 'fear' of, or apprehension about, a proposal, is a material consideration in determining an application (see *Gateshead MBC v S of S for the Environment* [1995] JPL 432, at 439 re 'public concern', and *West Midlands Probation Committee v S of S for the Environment and Walsall MBC* [1997] JPL 323, at 337 re 'fear'). These rulings have been confirmed by the Court of Appeal decision in *Newport Borough Council v Secretary of State for Wales and Another* [1998] JPL 377, at 378 where it was held that 'a perceived concern about safety is a material consideration which must be taken into account and given such weight as might be appropriate in the particular circumstances of the case'.

A further point made in the Vodafone letter (18.2.99) is that the proposed mast is 'set away from residential use'. Vodafone's judgement on this last point differs from that of my clients and other local residents who consider the site to be unacceptably close to their properties. My clients' house is approximately 82 metres from the proposed site. Lancaster Court Flats are stated by Vodafone to be only some 35 metres distant.

There appears to be a comparatively poor case for the proposed mast, combined with the strong probability that there are other sites in the locality where it could be located. These two factors have to be weighed against the fact that my clients and other local residents will (if the proposal proceeds) be subjected to emissions from the mast, about which they are justifiably most concerned, over a lengthy period almost certainly measured in decades.

This is a case where (in the words of PPG1, para 64) the application fails both the 'good neighbourliness' and 'fairness' tests, and ought in the 'public interest' to be refused because it would 'unacceptably affect amenities and the existing use of (residential) land and buildings'.

2 Martin Bacon to J.P., 25 March 1999

As this proposal is 'permitted development' the scope for the Council, as Local Planning Authority, to object is limited to the details of the siting and appearance of the pole, the antennae and the equipment cabin. Whilst the applicants have submitted details of 'need', this is generally a matter for them to determine and not for the Council to question. Health issues relating to telecommunications installations are not a 'material consideration' that can be taken into account by the Local Planning Authority, as explained in Planning Policy Guidance No. 8.

With regard to the notification to adjoining residents of such submissions as that at Nork Reservoir, there is no statutory requirement for this to be undertaken, although a Government circular does recommend it as good practice. To date the Council has not followed that advice, given resources, but your letter prompts me, as Chief Executive, to raise whether we should do so.[1]

3 R. N. Clifford to J.P., 7 April 1999

I do not agree that the local planning authority could have refused siting of the mast on grounds of the health fears expressed by and on behalf of local residents. Whilst I note your comments about 'fear', made in your letter of 22 March, I believe that the cases you cite were ones where the fear arose from an acknowledged problem, e.g. air pollution from an incinerator (Gateshead) and crime from the occupiers of an existing bail hostel proposed to be extended (Walsall). In contrast, the government's advice to local planning authorities is that the National Radiological Protection Board cannot provide any evidence to prove that health risks arise from telecommunication masts. Without any such evidence I do not see how the local planning authority could reasonably have held that a minimum 35 metres distance from the nearest dwelling was unacceptable.

---

[1] Martin Bacon has asked me to point out that letters from Council officials represent the position at the time they were written. There had been changes by April 2000. Most of these changes are reported elsewhere in this book.

I believe that the need for development is a matter for the code operator, and I cannot imagine why they would go to the expense of erecting a mast if it was not necessary. My understanding is that code operators need not only to be able to provide a signal at a specific location, but also to provide adequate capacity for their customers.

I conclude that whilst the Council's handling of the prior approval application may not have been to your clients' liking, no resident has been disadvantaged.

4 Nick Greer of Vodafone to Mary, 11 May 1999

Vodafone consider that the proposed site is acceptable in environmental terms, as agreed by Reigate and Banstead Council in their letter of 25 March 1999.

5 M. K. Caseley of Reigate and Banstead to Nick Greer, 14 May 1999

I am writing to clarify the fact that the Borough Council, as Local Planning Authority, did not purport to accept the proposal in environmental terms in the letter of 25 March 1999. That letter was in response to your company submitting a prior notification determination under the provisions of Class 24 of the Town and Country Planning (General Permitted Development) Order 1995 ... I trust that the above clarifies this matter.

APPENDIX C

Circular of 20 March 1999 to local residents

Nork Reservoir Telecommunications Apparatus

Vodafone intend to erect a 15+ metre mast in the reservoir (just behind the electricity station) to provide coverage for their network. It would be 35 metres from the flats. I have a copy of their 15 page 'notice of intention' sent to the Reigate and Banstead Council.

Local residents would lose from this installation, firstly, through the health hazard and, secondly, through the loss in value of their property. Health is the most serious matter. The health risk has not been proved or disproved; but many experts consider these rays dangerous and a potential cause of death. The loss in property value is mainly related to the health risk. Although residents of Lancaster Court and Green Curve are those most exposed to the dangers, the effects of these rays may extend over a wide area.

If we are to stop this installation, urgent action is required. I have written at length to the Chairman of Vodafone, the Chairman of Sutton and East Surrey Water and the Reigate and Banstead Council. PLEASE SUPPORT ME BY WRITING FIRST CLASS BY TOMORROW'S POST (SUNDAY) TO THE REIGATE AND BANSTEAD COUNCIL EXPRESSING YOUR CONCERN AND OPPOSITION. (Mr Caseley, Reigate and Banstead Council, Town Hall, Castlefield Road, Reigate, Surrey, RH20 0SH.)

Barry Bracewell-Milnes
26 Lancaster Court
Banstead

APPENDIX D

Letter of 25 March 1999 from BB-M to Brian Cowle

Urgent: can you help us 25/26 March. Delivered by hand

Nork Reservoir telecommunications apparatus

Congratulations to the Mayor Elect. In that capacity, can you help us on a matter of the utmost urgency?

Reigate and Banstead Council did not inform us (as they could and should have done) about Vodafone's intention to install a mast emitting rays some 35 metres or less from these flats. We heard about the matter by chance on 15 March. Since then I have written to the Chairman of Vodafone and Sutton and East Surrey Water and to Reigate and Banstead Council (20 March, copies enclosed; none has had the courtesy to reply), collected 124 signatures from residents (less than ten of whom refused to sign), reported these 124 signatures to Vodafone and Sutton and East Surrey (also to Mr. Caseley via Councillor Selby) and written twice to the Prime Minister and John Prescott. Sir Archibald Hamilton MP has written to John Fooks, Chairman of Sutton and East Surrey, in support of my letter. Other weighty representations have to my knowledge been made to Mr Caseley.

I understand (today, 25 March) that Mr. Caseley is

minded to ignore all these representations and 'terminate' (that is, say yes to Vodafone) on the ground that it is much too late to do otherwise. But whose fault is that? Mr. Caseley ensured that we were not informed earlier.

Although opposition to this mast is running at more than ten to one (much of it passionate) on a statistically significant sample of 124 signatures (collected in one day, which is in itself remarkable), most of our options for legal redress are blocked. I am taking advice on the possibilities of physical protest and have so advised Sir Archibald Hamilton. (Please do not tell Vodafone this).

In my opinion, Reigate and Banstead officials have made a horrible hash of this whole business. I shall of course go to the Local Ombudsman; by an interesting coincidence, Reigate and Banstead have just put a helpful leaflet through my door explaining precisely how to do this. I would not doubt that the Ombudsman would criticise Reigate and Banstead.

It is ridiculous to argue that it is too late to do anything when the mast is not yet erected. Can you telephone Mr. Caseley or (preferably) his hierarchical superiors this evening 25 March?

APPENDIX E

Letter of 23 March 1999 from BB-M to Sir Archibald Hamilton

Nork Reservoir telecommunications apparatus

I enclose letters of 20 March to the Chairman of Vodafone, the Chairman of Sutton and East Surrey Water and Reigate and Banstead Borough Council and also a note distributed to local residents.

I collected 124 signatures in a single day on Sunday 21 March urging Reigate and Banstead Council to do everything possible to prevent this installation. It would have been well over 200 if everyone had been in. I wonder how often your own canvassing has enjoyed this level of support. Many signatories were mobile phone users, as we are. Respondents refusing to sign for reasons of disagreement were fewer than ten.

I note from the Epsom, Banstead and Leatherhead Informer of 18 March that Mr. de Robillard is reported as saying that he has had help from you in his campaign against Cellnet's mast in Ruxley Lane, Ewell. I hope that you will help us, and I should like to know how you propose to do so. It is more to the point to try to prevent a mast from going up than to try to have it demolished once it has been erected.

Any help you can give us could serve to reduce a debt

of obligation. Vodafone's notice of intention to Reigate and Banstead says that their licence was granted in 1983. They mention the Telecommunications Act 1984; the Town and Country Planning (General Permitted Development) Order 1995 Schedule 2, Part 24; the Telecommunications Prior Approval Procedures Code of Best Practice March 1996 Part 2.1(ii); PPG8 December 1992 (as amended); Sections 19 and 22 and the General Development Order Consolidation Circular 9/95 Appendix E (June 1995). All this legislation assisting Vodafone to bombard us for 24 hours a day with cancerous rays (and without even notifying us in advance) was passed under the last Conservative Administration. If you ever wonder why the Conservatives lost so heavily in 1997, this may provide a clue.

Unsolicited comments from respondents to my request for signatures included the following: 'It's disgraceful we weren't informed'; 'Government's all for big business and to hell with the residents'; 'what is this country coming to?' A cause of particular amazement was that Vodafone can do this without planning permission whereas a householder has to get planning permission to build a garden shed or break through a party wall. I forebore to reply that for this unholy mess we had to thank the last Conservative Government in general and you, as our MP, in particular; but my more alert respondents were aware that it was the Conservatives who had made it so difficult for us to fight a company like Vodafone, and several said so in tones of undisguised contempt.

I regard myself as something of a hardline libertarian (to the right of Attila the Hun, as they say); but my concept of property rights stops well short of an owner's freedom to bombard his neighbours with poisonous rays.

Fighting your legacy of the Vodafone mast is now my top priority. If I can interest the national Press, so much the better. I shall not point the finger of blame at the Conservatives; but if others do so, that is not my principal concern.

William Hague is apparently trying to distance himself

from his predecessors of 1979–1997, and I read reports of his apologising for things that in my opinion require no apology. But here is something in a different category. If he were to say 'We can now see that we made a horrible mistake and we shall urge Labour to change the ground rules', he might win back some of the lost supporters who continue to remain so elusive.

Urgent action is required. What can you do this week?

Postscript to letter of 23 March to Sir Archibald Hamilton

I understand that Mr Caseley is reluctant to listen to representations. The matter is urgent, since the mast could go up within days. I am considering sending the papers to the Prime Minister and the Secretary of State for the Environment; but I should like to give you a chance to respond before I do so. I am coming to London today to deliver this letter by hand. Could you say something by return, please?

APPENDIX F

Letter of 24 March 1999 from BB-M to the Prime Minister

Urgent appeal for help: can you act today 25 March?

Dear Prime Minister,

    Nork Reservoir telecommunications apparatus

Can you help us? You are our last hope.

Vodafone are proposing to erect a 15+ metre telecommunications mast 25 (rather than 35) metres from these flats. Planning permission is not required. No one was obliged to inform us or did so. I learnt of the matter by chance.

I enclose copies of my letters of 20 March to the Chairman of Vodafone, the Chairman of Sutton and East Surrey Water and Reigate and Banstead Council. None has had the courtesy to reply.

124 signatures to a petition to the Council were collected on 21 March. This is a high level of support on any topic. Fewer than ten refused to sign. Reigate and Banstead Council have had dozens of letters of protest. But this degree of opposition counts for nothing. We are stitched up by the legislation (which is specified in the postscript to this letter).

Although I believe in capitalism and the free market, the behaviour of Vodafone and Sutton and East Surrey Water are way off the chart. All the 124 signatories are customers of Sutton and East Surrey Water, which has not even replied to me. Would you be willing to send a message to John Fooks, Chairman of Sutton and East Surrey Water, asking him to desist from the agreement with Vodafone, and to Lord MacLaurin, Chairman of Vodafone, asking him to put the operation on hold, which is what I have asked both these gentlemen to do? They would, of course, take more notice of you than they have taken of me. If you did so, I am sure your move would be warmly welcomed, not only by Nork residents but by the country at large, and would attract immense publicity.

This mast could go up on Monday or even earlier. Can you act before the weekend?

APPENDIX G

Letter of 25 March 1999 from BB-M to the Prime Minister

Urgent: can you help us on 26 March?

Dear Prime Minister,

      Nork Reservoir telecommunications apparatus

I refer to my letter of yesterday 24 March. I hope that your office has already been in touch with Lord MacLaurin, Chairman of Vodafone, and Mr. John Fooks, Chairman of Sutton and East Surrey Water.

Vodafone's Notice of Intention to Reigate and Banstead Council of 19 February (of which I have a copy) says: 'Purpose of development: to provide in-building and portable coverage for the Vodafone GSM network for the A2022/217 junction which is currently lacking due to inadequate network coverage and network capacity'. 'In-building coverage' presumably means coverage for local residents, who (on a statistically significant sample of 124 signatures collected in a single day) are against the installation by a margin of more than ten to one, many of them passionately so. If 'portable coverage' means coverage for motorists, the use of mobile phones by motorists was banned by the revised Highway Code on 27 February, eight days after Vodafone submitted their Notice of Intention to Reigate and Banstead. The A2022/217 junction is the busiest for miles around, and the use of mobiles by motorists in the vicinity would be criminally reckless. If 'portable coverage' means use by visiting pedestrians, why are they so important? Why should we be so put about for their convenience?

Given the strength of the opposition to this installation, which is known to Vodafone and to Sutton and East Surrey, I believe that a call from your office expressing interest in the matter would be enough to persuade the two companies to put the matter on hold. If this has not already been done, **I urge that such a call be made from your office before the close of business on 26 March**. Monday could be too late.

May I please have a reply by the weekend?

APPENDIX H

Letter of 26 March 1999 from BB-M to the Prime Minister

Urgent: can you help us?

Dear Prime Minister,

    Nork Reservoir telecommunications apparatus

I refer to my letters to you of 24 and 25 March.

Reigate and Banstead Council decided last night to 'terminate' (that is, to let the Vodafone application go ahead). The decision was taken by paid officials despite representations from the local Councillor. The officials omitted to inform residents of the proposal to install this mast, although they could have done so. Residents first heard of the proposal by chance early last week. By this time the arrangement between Vodafone and Reigate and Banstead Council was far advanced. The officials seem to have decided that Vodafone would go to appeal if turned down and that it would be easier for them to override the wishes of the residents than to turn down Vodafone.

The decision has not been taken on the merits of the case. There is no mistaking the strength of the opposition to this mast. 124 signatures and dozens of letters have reached the officials. Fewer than ten residents refused to sign. None of these letters has been answered. A five-page representation written by an environmental expert and arguing against the Vodafone application on technical and legal grounds was submitted by a neighbour of mine on 22 March; the official who reported the Council's decision to this neighbour by telephone last night admitted in a jocular manner that he had not read this representation.

The basic problem is the secondary legislation specified in the postscript to my letter to you of 24 March. Vodafone and Reigate and Banstead officials have been acting within this legislation. They can afford to do so. The legislation systematically blocks the residents' means of legal objection and redress. Nobody is obliged to pay any attention to their wishes nor to the strength of their legal arguments.

Our situation is desperate. We face being bombarded 24 hours a day for the rest of our lives with rays that many of us believe to be cancerous (although we recognise that others, mostly living at a safe distance, think otherwise). We cannot leave because we are financial prisoners: few, if any, of us would have bought our flats here if we had known about this mast and other prospective purchasers must be expected to feel the same. It is a life sentence, perhaps shortened if our fears about cancer prove to be correct. By that time, the officials who have condemned us to this fate will be living elsewhere on index-linked pensions.

The behaviour of Vodafone and Sutton and East Surrey Water give a bad name to capitalism in general and the privatised utilities in particular. The conduct of Sutton and East Surrey is especially remarkable, since all their victims are also their customers and since the fee for their betrayal is believed to be a derisory £5,000 a year, which a single determined individual might be willing to pay. I put this suggestion to Mr. John Fooks, Chairman of Sutton and East Surrey Water in my letter of 20 March, copied to you on 24 March. I have had no reply.

APPENDIX I

Letter of 27 March 1999 from BB-M to the Prime Minister

Dear Prime Minister,

    Nork Reservoir telecommunications apparatus

I refer to my letters to you of 24, 25 and 26 March. These were all marked 'Urgent: can you help us?', and I hope that you have done so. The present letter has a longer timescale and raises a policy question which you may find of interest.

Door-to-door canvassing is not usually much fun, as I am sure you will agree. But I enjoyed my hard work last Sunday because (apart from the eight recusants) I was warmly welcomed wherever I went, by mobile phone owners like myself as well as by others. It may well be that I have done more market research on this subject than Vodafone have, and perhaps I can help them here. The overwhelming reaction from my 124 respondents was one of relief that at last they had the opportunity to tell someone how much they hated these masts as a threat to the value of their property and above all as a potential cancer hazard. Some signed cheerfully in a matter-of-fact way; others were emotional and passionate on the subject. I understand from Reigate and Banstead Council that they received about a hundred letters of protest. This is a large number, especially as the canvassing was done on one day, mostly by me, and only eight days elapsed between my acquiring a copy of Vodafone's proposal and Reigate and Banstead's decision to 'terminate' (grant approval).

A number of my more alert respondents told me that resistance was hopeless because of the way in which the secondary legislation had been drafted. Vodafone are probably used to ignoring the opinions of local residents and trampling on their feelings and interests. Near Nork Reservoir there were by good fortune two individuals able and willing to act and possessing some of the necessary background. This does not always happen. There is no reason why opinion in the houses and flats I canvassed should be exceptional; I would expect it to be replicated across much of the country.

The purpose of the Vodafone mast is 'to provide in-building and portable coverage for the Vodafone GSM network for the A2022/A217 junction which is currently lacking due to inadequate network coverage and network capacity'. Outside the ranks of the eight recusants, I found no sympathy for this purpose. Nobody complained of inadequate network coverage or inadequate network capacity. Everybody was concerned about having a new mast in the vicinity. Similarly, there was no diminution of support as I moved further away from the site of the proposed installation. It seems that Vodafone are pursuing the interest of a small minority including themselves (less than one in ten) against the wishes of the large majority.

It follows that what my respondents wanted was, not to have the mast resited, but to have it banned. There was no NIMBY factor. Nobody wanted to protect his interests at the expense of his neighbours. Everybody wanted to protect his interests at the expense of Vodafone. This aspect of the matter is of particular concern to me. I collected fifteen signatures from the Basing Road estate immediately to the east of the A217. I am bound in honour to these people. A woman on the Basing Road estate said that she was deeply and totally opposed to Vodafone's masts but that she would not sign my petition for fear of having a mast even nearer to her home than in the original plan. A company like Vodafone might indeed seek an escape from the present mess by resiting the mast further away from these flats and nearer to the Basing Road estate. I could not be party to such an arrangement. I do not wish to protect my interests at the expense of my neighbours on the Basing Road estate. The public interest requires that Vodafone should give way, not that one group of neighbours should contend with another.

I am not a hardline socialist; but the behaviour of Vodafone and Sutton and East Surrey Water are way off my chart. They cannot seem to grasp the idea that the activities of large public companies, not least public utilities, require public tolerance and acceptance. If a company persistently affronts public opinion, its activities may be curtailed or even banned.

Friends of the Earth Scotland have a policy on telecommunications masts and I have seen their papers. The logical goal is a total ban on new masts; followed by a policy of economising on existing masts.

My experience strongly suggests that such policies could be a political vote-winner.

APPENDIX J

Letter of 20 March 1999 from BB-M to John Fooks, Chairman of Sutton and East Surrey Water PLC (SESW)

PERSONAL

Nork Reservoir telecommunications apparatus

I enclose a copy of my letter of today's date to Lord MacLaurin of Knebworth, Chairman of Vodafone.

I have lived in these flats for more than thirty years and been a customer of yours throughout this period. I take it very unkindly that you should have gone behind the backs of residents to make an arrangement with a firm that had no previous connection with this site. You have not been in touch with residents of these flats nor with the ground landlords. Even minor courtesies have not been observed.

Every time you send me a bill, it is accompanied by documents parading your company's social conscience. Your behaviour in the matter of Nork Reservoir shows what a sham such talk is.

If it is true that Vodafone are paying you as little as £5,000 a year, you have not been very clever either. I would expect the loss in value per property in these flats and adjoining roads as a result of the mast to be not less than £1,000 per property, perhaps much more. So the total loss you are inflicting on your customers and neighbours is a large multiple of your paltry fee for betraying us. You have not even looked into the question of whether the interested parties here would be able and willing to outbid Vodafone. £5,000 a year is the sort of sum a single determined owner might be willing to provide; it could be less than the annual loss on his house.

If you have any discretion left at this late stage, I ask you to countermand the arrangement with Vodafone. If you have not, we shall have to continue the fight on other fronts.

The privatised utilities have not always enjoyed a good reputation recently. Although some of the criticism has been unfair, a matter like Nork Reservoir helps me to understand why a number of privatised utilities have earned themselves a bad name. Your name could deteriorate as a result of this. I urge you to do everything in your power to resile from this disastrous arrangement.

I am sending this letter by registered post.

APPENDIX K

Letter of 20 March 1999 from BB-M to Lord MacLaurin of Knebworth, Chairman of Vodafone PLC

PERSONAL

**Nork Reservoir, Brighton Road, Banstead, Surrey
OS Grid reference 524663 160179
Notice of intention to install telecommunications apparatus**

**Your reference AL/CS4754
Your date 19 February 1999**

A copy of your notice of intention has just come into my hands. I am writing immediately to express the grave concern of my neighbours and myself. They can speak for themselves later.
(1) Our principal concern is the health risk. A substantial body of expert opinion regards mobile phones as dangerous to their users. My family owns a mobile phone but scarcely ever uses it, for reasons of health. If the use of mobile phones is dangerous, 24 hour-a-day exposure to rays emitted by a nearby telecommunications mast must be much worse. These anxieties are already in the public

domain. Thirty years ago, asbestos was not considered dangerous; now it is a prohibited substance. A substantial body of opinion regards the rays from telecommunications masts as coming into a similar category. If present anxieties about telecommunications rays are confirmed, companies like yours could be pursued for amounts similar to those being paid out by tobacco companies at present.
(2) I should not have bought property in these flats if there had been a telecommunications mast next door. Many potential purchasers are of the same opinion. A mast must reduce the value of these flats.
(3)   The 'purpose of development is to provide in-building and portable coverage for the Vodafone GSM network for the A2022/A217 junction which is currently lacking due to inadequate network coverage and network capacity'. (Point 3 on unnumbered page 12 of your document.) This junction is the busiest for miles around. As far as I know, a motorist's use of a mobile in such a place (or anywhere) is either illegal or officially discouraged. I would regard it as criminally reckless to use a mobile within several hundred yards of this junction, which I know well, having lived in this area all my life.
(4)   Unnumbered page 2 of your document says 'The site at Nork reservoir in the opinion of Vodafone ... is set away from residential use'. However, unnumbered page 12 says: 'Location of and distance to nearest residential property: Lancaster Court Flats, approximately 35m distant'. If one of your installations were sited 35 metres from the home of one of your directors, I wonder whether it would still be 'the opinion of Vodafone' that this installation was 'set away from residential use'. Such use of language brings Vodafone into serious disrepute and, given your importance on the Stock Exchange, is a matter of public concern and even of national interest.
(5)   The criteria you quote under 'Policy' on unnumbered page 9 have been overtaken by events; this part of your document is dated 17 April 1996. I understand that there

has been a recent High Court case that bears on this matter and that you would be ill advised to proceed without researching this case. My neighbour, Dr. Mary Saunders, of 63 Green Curve, will be delivering a letter to Reigate and Banstead Council on this subject on Monday, 22 March.

(6) I note from a recent newspaper report that the residents of Ruxley Lane, Ewell are campaigning to have a Cellnet mast removed. Whatever the rights and wrongs of that argument, it might have been better for all parties if the matter had been more thoroughly discussed beforehand.

I am therefore writing to ask you to put this development on hold, in order to spare both Vodafone and the residents of Lancaster Court what could be a long dispute. In the short time at my disposal, I have made contact with a lawyer who works full time in this area and tells me that the residents have a good case.

I am sending this letter by registered post.

APPENDIX L

Circular of 28 March 1999 from BB-M to residents of Nork Way, Warren Road and Fir Tree Road

URGENT: CAN YOU ACT TODAY, 28 MARCH, PLEASE?

NORK RESERVOIR TELECOMMUNICATIONS APPARATUS

Vodafone propose to erect a mast on land owned by Sutton and East Surrey Water PLC at Nork Reservoir. The mast would be about 100 feet from these flats, and it would emit rays 24 hours a day for the foreseeable future over a wide area. Although opinion is divided, more and more experts believe these rays to be hazardous to health or even life-threatening. The effect on property values could be severe.

Neither Vodafone, Sutton and East Surrey, nor Reigate and Banstead Council informed any member of the public about this proposal. Reigate and Banstead officials did not even inform their Councillors. I learnt about the matter by chance. Vodafone's plans first came into my hands on 17 March. Reigate and Banstead received a petition on 22 March signed by 124 people. They also received about 100 letters of protest. They turned us down on 25 March.

Although residents of Lancaster Court are in the front line of this battle, the Vodafone mast affects all recipients of this letter. In the course of collecting 124 signatures I noticed no diminution of support as I moved away from the proposed site of the mast. Mobile phone owners were generally as willing to sign as non-owners. I had less than ten refusals. The overwhelming response I had was that it is not enough to resite this mast: we do not want it anywhere.

Since Reigate and Banstead are against us, we are appealing to Sutton and East Surrey Water. YOU CAN HELP. Would you please write to John Fooks, Chairman, Sutton and East Surrey Water PLC, London Road, Redhill, Surrey, RH1 1LJ. Please post first-class by tomorrow, Monday 29 March. Two or three lines would be enough, expressing your opposition. There is no need for arguments or explanations. You might add that all victims of this mast are customers of Sutton and East Surrey Water and that the company should have more consideration for its customers. A copy to me would be welcome but is not essential. PLEASE ACT TODAY. Every letter counts.

APPENDIX M

Letter of 28 March 1999 from BB-M to Phil Holder, Managing Director, SESW

Nork Reservoir telecommunications apparatus

Thank you for your letter of 26 March covering a copy of the letter of the same date from your Chairman to Sir Archibald Hamilton, MP. I am replying briefly so as to catch today's post. I and others have much more to say later.

The letter from John Fooks to Sir Archibald reads in large part like a form letter. It is helpful to have this explanation of your position on telecommunications masts. This general position is entirely inappropriate to the particularities of Nork Reservoir, which your Chairman's letter does not address. I mention only three points here.

First, your Chairman does not refer to the 124 signatures to the protest against the mast, collected in less than a day, mostly by me. I was welcomed with open arms almost everywhere I went. The welcome did not cool as I moved away from the proposed site of the mast. Less than 10 refused to sign. There were about 100 letters of protest to Reigate and Banstead. I understand that this is above average. You might like to check with your Chairman's office on Monday 29 March in case he has had any correspondence on the subject from local residents.

Second, your policy of leaving 'the decision as to

whether or not there should be a mast to the local council which has been elected to represent the interests of the residents' has not in this instance been a great success. Reigate and Banstead officials have made an unholy mess of the whole business. I and others will be happy to substantiate this at length. Here I merely say that before the officials (not the Councillors 'elected to represent the interests of the residents') formally 'terminated' (that is, passed) the proposal from Vodafone, one of their messengers posted through my letterbox a 'complaint form' accompanied by a leaflet entitled 'Complaints procedure: your right to complain'. This piece of self-incrimination is the only thing these officials have got right.

Third, I have probably done more door-to-door canvassing on this subject in the last week than you have done in the whole of your life. If you doubt what I say, I strongly recommend that you conduct a personal canvass in this area asking respondents whether they favour the connivance of Sutton and East Surrey in the rape of this neighbourhood by Vodafone masts. None of my respondents want the mast resited: all of them want it banned.

As it happens, I was the consultant who drafted the representations of the Institute of Directors to the Conservative Government of the day arguing for the privatisation of the Water Boards. This was a way-out idea at the time, and the IoD was years ahead of other representative bodies. I am aghast at the monster I have helped to create.

I have not yet sent a copy of this letter to the Prime Minister.

APPENDIX N

Letter of 29 March 1999 from BB-M to Phil Holder, Managing Director, SESW

Nork Reservoir telecommunications apparatus

When I wrote to you yesterday 28 March, I said that there was much more to say. This letter is the first instalment.

Nowadays cases of injustice and maladministration are two-a-penny. It can be difficult to catch the attention of Ministers, journalists and the general public, however strong the victims' arguments. That is where visual aids come in.

By an interesting coincidence, the same day that I wrote to you the Sunday Telegraph carried a humorous cartoon which so perfectly captured the present situation that it deserves a wider circulation. Accompanied by a new caption and a lively commentary, it could attract widespread attention from the local Press. The national Press might be interested as well.

Copyright should be no problem. I know the Editor of the Sunday Telegraph, Dominic Lawson, and I have no doubt that he would help us. His newspaper carries a weekly column on cases like these.

I apologise for the quality of the cartoon, which is a photocopy of a cutting from the Sunday Telegraph. Don't worry: the job of circulating the cartoon would be done at a fully professional level.

I am sending a copy to my MP, Sir Archibald Hamilton, who may share my opinion that it would have been more polite of your Chairman, Mr. John Fooks, to answer his letter instead of sending a form letter that made no reference to the particularities of Nork Reservoir.

I am also sending copies to Lord MacLaurin, Chairman of Vodafone, and Mr. John Fooks. These gentlemen have been too busy to reply to my letters; but I hope that they will find time to join in the fun. I am sure they enjoy a joke at their own expense.

I am not yet sending a copy to the Prime Minister. He has been heavily preoccupied in the last few days and may not have had time to read my letters. I am confident that the cartoon would at least catch the attention of his officials.

I am sure that circulating this cartoon is entirely legal. However, if Sutton and East Surrey Water think otherwise and decide to sue me for libel, I shall endure this ordeal as patiently as I can.

*'So, does anyone else feel that
their needs aren't being met?'*

© The New Yorker Collection 1997 Tom Cheney from cartoonbank.com. All Rights Reserved.

THIS IS HOW SUTTON AND EAST SURREY WATER TREATS ITS CUSTOMERS

The *Sunday Telegraph*, 28 March 1999

APPENDIX O

Letter of 30 March 1999 from BB-M to John Fooks, Chairman, SESW

Nork Reservoir telecommunications apparatus

If your company is engaged in discussions on this subject over the next day or two, I hope that whoever speaks for the residents will not sell the pass. That would have unfortunate consequences for all concerned.

The officials of Reigate and Banstead Council have aggravated the problem by not informing the residents (apparently to save on delivery costs) or even their own Councillors (which would have cost nothing).

If the Residents' Association are minded to compromise, they do not speak for the residents.

During the last few days I have visited nearly 1,000 homes in Nork and the Basing Road estate and Banstead Road (where I used to live). I may be better informed about local opinion than some others are.

Resiting is not an acceptable option. We just want to get this contraption right out of the Nork and Basing Road and Banstead Road area.

There is no NIMBY factor. We do not wish to solve our problems at the expense of neighbours across the boundary.

Quality of reception is not a concern. Only one respondent complained about quality. Several said: if the quality is bad (which we doubt) the user should move on or use a corded telephone. Practically everyone rated quality of life above quality of reception. We just want to be left in peace.

Vodafone could be well advised to put on hold any plans to erect new masts within many miles of here.

APPENDIX P

Letter of 7 April 1999 from BB-M to Lord MacLaurin of Knebworth, Chairman of Vodafone PLC

CONFIDENTIAL

Nork Reservoir telecommunications apparatus

Although Vodafone did not give us advance warning of the proposal to erect a mast, I should like to deal more courteously with you. So you may wish to be apprised of our latest thoughts.

The attached cartoon is being given a limited circulation at present, as is indicated below. Please respect its confidentiality.

Public opinion in this area is hostile to the erection of a Vodafone mast anywhere in Nork reservoir or anywhere in Nork. IT IS ALSO HOSTILE TO ADDITIONAL VODAFONE CAPACITY BY WHATEVER MEANS FOR AT LEAST A MILE IN ANY DIRECTION FROM THE SITE ORIGINALLY PROPOSED IN NORK RESERVOIR.

If your staff are engaged in discussions with the water company or other third parties over the next days and weeks, you might like to bring local opinion here to the attention of your spokesmen.

Copies: Mr John Fooks, Chairman, Sutton and East Surrey Water PLC

Mr Dominic Lawson, Editor, The Sunday Telegraph. Your cartoons have been a godsend

Mr John Smith, Artful Plans Ltd

CONFIDENTIAL
Mr. Dominic Lawson – please keep on hold

'Very well put, Harper'

©The New Yorker Collection 1999 Gahan Wilson from cartoonbank.com. All rights reserved.

The *Sunday Telegraph*, 4 April 1999

This is how Vodafone treats a resident protesting against a Vodafone mast

Mr John Smith, Artful Plans Ltd

APPENDIX Q

Circular of 7 May 1999 from Mary Saunders

NORK VODAFONE TELECOMMUNICATIONS MAST

Important - Please Write a Thank you Letter

You will all no doubt have heard the good news by now. A few days ago Sutton and East Surrey Water asked Vodafone to 'look elsewhere' for a site for the mast. This is an extremely welcome outcome.

The decision was taken by Mr Holder, the Managing Director of Sutton and East Surrey Water. Historically, reservoir sites (being on high ground) have always been used for telecommunications masts for the essential services. This policy has more recently been expanded to included masts for mobile phones if these have been approved by the council (who have very little choice in the matter). The refusal of the mast was not an easy decision for him to make, and it was made largely as a result of the letters of objection written mainly by residents from Lancaster Court, Eastgate and Green Curve.

Nobody has had any right to see the measurements that Vodafone made when they applied for this mast originally, so it has been impossible to assess the 'need' for this particular application at this particular site. It may be that in their view the need was very great (for in-car use at the

Banstead cross roads) and the site they chose was in their view the only possible one. If this is their opinion they will soon be back to Sutton and East Surrey Water offering a financial sum that the Water Company might find hard to refuse. Other telecommunications companies may also approach Sutton and East Surrey Water in the future.

If Mr Holder receives sufficient letters of thanks then I am sure that he will stick by his decision for good. If, on the other hand, nobody bothers to thank him, then there still is a remote possibility that we still might have a mast somewhere on the water board land.

Please could you write a thank you letter now. A very brief note is all that is required.

Please address your letter of thanks to:
Mr P B Holder
Managing Director
Sutton and East Surrey Water PLC
London Road
Redhill
Surrey RH1 1LJ

APPENDIX R

*Ruxley Lane: Contribution from
Councillor Mrs Jean Smith*

Together with a local resident, Dr. Rolf Bachen, I have been battling for nearly a year against the erection of telecommunication masts near hospitals, schools and residential homes.

Unfortunately the mast in Ruxley Lane was erected under Permitted Development which means that the Local Authority is powerless to refuse permission because it is not more than 15 metres high. Only appearance and site are of material consideration and the company only has to say there is no other suitable site and that they will plant trees around the mast to comply with planning law.

That deals with the visual impact, but of much greater concern is the perceived health hazard posed by these masts. We are in a Catch 22 situation. The Health & Safety Executive and telecommunication companies rely on the guidance laid down by the National Radiological Protection Board (N.R.P.B.) who stubbornly refuse to change their guidelines in the face of serious challenge from eminent scientists. In England the masts are considered safe until proved dangerous whereas in the U.S.A. and New Zealand the reverse applies and they are deemed harmful until proved safe.

The N.R.P.B. itself has said several times that further

research is needed. Tessa Jowell, Minister for Public Health, and Richard Caborn, Minister for Planning, have both acknowledged the need for more research, as have many leading scientists such as Sir Richard Doll, Professor Henry Lai of the University of Washington and Dr. G. Hyland, Senior Lecturer in Theoretical Physics at Warwick University. Dr. Hyland gave evidence to the Government's Science and Technology Committee about the non-thermal health hazard of telecommunication masts and drew attention to 'the inadequacy of existing safety guidelines governing the exposure of the public to radiation of the kind used in mobile telephony, and to the fact that the philosophy underlying the formulation of these guidelines is fundamentally flawed'. He pointed to the 'numerous reports (that display a remarkable consistency world-wide) of adverse health effects experienced by people resident in the vicinity of the base stations, the most common complaints being those of a neurological nature, such as effects on short term memory, concentration, learning, sleep disorder and anxiety states, as well as increases in the incidence of leukaemia'.

The mast causing concern to my residents in Ruxley Lane is only 40 metres away from the homes of several of them, including that of Dr. Bachen. I therefore arranged for a meeting with BT Cellnet to discuss their fears. They sent along their Health and Safety Executive who was very pleasant and listened carefully and even made a site visit. However, two months later all we received was a letter promising cosmetic improvements to the appearance by more tree planting and an acoustic panel to reduce the noise level. 'It's good to talk' they say, but not, it seems, to my residents!

One must of course accept the need to encourage commercial enterprise, but this should not take precedence over people's health and safety.

Until the outcome of the research is published, therefore, I strongly suggest that Local Government should be given greater powers to control the siting of masts up to

15 metres and that a firm policy should be issued now regarding the minimum distance of these masts from residential buildings, schools and hospitals. It is disgraceful that such a policy does not exist.

JEAN SMITH
EPSOM & EWELL BOROUGH COUNCILLOR
November 1999

APPENDIX S

Letter of 2 June 1999 from BB-M to R. N. Clifford, Director of Environmental Services, Reigate and Banstead Borough Council

Application 99 P/0674

Telecom Securicor Cellular Radio Ltd; BBM

This responds to your form letter of 26 May addressed to me as 'Dear Sir/Madam'. I am not a madam and I have not addressed you as 'Dear Sir/Madam'.
(1) I met Hamish Watson at the Banstead Help Shop on Monday 24 May. He provided me with a two-page photocopy of an application of 18 January 1999 on behalf of Telecom Securicor Cellular Radio Ltd.
(2) In a letter dated 26 May, Nigel Griffiths, Director and Company Secretary of Securicor PLC, says: 'The Company Secretary of BT Cellnet has confirmed to me that the mast in question is a Cellnet one and has nothing to do with Securicor'. So two questions arise:- (a) If the mast in question has nothing to do with Securicor, why is the name of Securicor included in the application of 18 January and your letter of 26 May? (b) If the mast in question is a Cellnet one (Securicor's letter of 26 May), why is there practically no relationship between "Cellnet' and the name

of the applicant in your letter of the same date? Are the status and bona fides of the applicant in good order?

(3)   Hamish Watson explained on 24 May that the original application of 18 January was soon to be superseded. I take it that this had happened before you sent your letter of 26 May. There are three car parks at BBM/Banstead Station. The first is immediately adjacent to the road from Banstead to Ewell which goes past Banstead Station; it is apparently designed for setting down and picking up and has about three spaces. The second is at the same level and occupies the space of the former station master's house's back garden. The third is at the lower level of the railway (thirty-nine pedestrian steps down). As I understand the matter from Hamish Watson, the applicant wishes to change the mast from one in the third car park on a platform to one in the second car park without a platform, the overall height remaining the same.

(4)   Hamish Watson further explained that an application that had already been 'determined' (agreed) could not be modified, so that the process had to start again from the beginning; this is apparently what is happening now.

(5)   You may remember a recent proposal by Vodafone to erect a mast in Nork Reservoir. This was agreed by Reigate and Banstead Council despite fierce opposition by local residents. The proposal was eventually abandoned because Sutton and East Surrey Water PLC withdrew permission for their land to be used for this purpose. Sutton and East Surrey Water have shown some concern for the interests of Nork residents; Reigate and Banstead Borough Council have so far shown no such concern for us.

(6)   The considerations for Nork Reservoir and BBM are very similar. Both sites are on the boundaries of Nork. They are within a few hundred yards of each other. Both affect the same residents of Nork, although the rays would be beamed on them from slightly different angles. Both would devalue property over a wide area.

(7)   Although the interests, wishes and health of Nork residents may be of little concern to you, I may know more

about opinion here than anyone, since I canvassed much of the area myself. I can report (a) that opinion among mobile phone users and non-users alike was more than ten-to-one against any further masts and (b) that this hostility did not diminish as I moved away from the Nork Reservoir site.

(8) BBM Banstead Station is immediately adjacent to Banstead Downs, which constitutes or includes a Site of Special Scientific Interest. It is legal hair-splitting to say that this argument is unimportant because the mast would be a few yards away from the Downs. Has English Nature been consulted? (Telecommunications Prior Approval Procedures Code of Best Practice, page 32).

(9) The mast at BBM would be an eyesore on a prominent local landmark.

(10) You may be ill advised to say that 'health issues are not a matter upon which the Local Planning Authority can comment'. The World Health Organisation Draft Document of 1998 on Electromagnetic Fields (Philip Chadwick and Zenon Sienkiewicz) says, among much else: 'The topic is especially controversial and there is often much confusion caused by conflicting findings' (Page 9). 'The European Commission's Expert Group on this issue states that definitive answers about health hazards are unlikely in the short term' (Page 18). If you have not seen this WHO document, I strongly advise you to obtain a copy.

(11) Public concern on this subject has been mounting in recent years. Many people do not wish to be proved right by dying of cancer. If you ever read the newspapers, you will see that the danger of these rays is a weekly or even a daily topic.

(12) Your dismissal of the Gateshead (1995) and Walsall (1997) and Newport Borough Council (1998) judgments may thus be ill founded. These judgments still stand as precedents, and the field of their potential application is steadily increasing as a result of findings adverse to the safety of these rays. National and local government may be slow off the mark; but the courts can take cognisance

of events on the previous day. Reigate and Banstead Council could be on weak or very weak ground if they ignored the perceived anxieties of the residents who pay their officials' salaries.

I therefore ask Reigate and Banstead Borough Council to withhold permission for the erection of a mast at BBM.

APPENDIX T

Letter of 1 May 1999 from BB-M to Banstead Builders' Merchants (BBM)

Dear Sirs,

Securicor mast at BBM

It has just come to my notice that Securicor intend to erect a telecommunications mast on Banstead Builders' Merchants land at Banstead Station and that this proposal passed through the hands of Reigate and Banstead Borough Council some time ago.

I understand that the mast has not yet been erected and thus that its erection requires the continuing support of both Securicor and BBM. That is why I am writing.

A recent proposal to erect a Vodafone mast on Sutton and East Surrey Water PLC property at Nork Reservoir aroused deep opposition over an extensive area among mobile phone users and non-users alike. Opinion was ten-to-one against a mast on any terms. Opposition did not diminish further away from the proposed site.

A Securicor mast at Banstead Station would be just as bad and would affect much the same area. The damage done to local residents would be a large multiple of the fee of a few thousand pounds that is normally paid to the landowner in these circumstances. The damage done to me alone would be more than this normal fee, let alone the damage done to others.

I do not know whether BBM has any wish to be a good neighbour to local residents. If it has, it should resile from this disastrous arrangement with Securicor forthwith. But, even if it has no wish to be a good neighbour, I am willing to match the fee that Securicor have offered you on condition that their mast is not built. You would thus not lose financially.

I am sending this letter by recorded delivery (RT933864105 GB).

APPENDIX U

*Letter of 14 June 1999 from BB-M
to Nicholas Eldred*

Company Secretary, BT Cellnet

Mast at BBM

Thank you very much for your courteous and informative letter of 7 June. Your letter and recent correspondence from Mr. Nigel Griffiths of Securicor make a pleasant change from the curt form letters and silences that I have had from other parties on the subject of the proposed Vodafone mast at Nork Reservoir.

I do not dispute your account of the matter, except that you say that you have taken into account local sensibilities. On this subject I can provide background of which you may not be aware.

Earlier this year, Vodafone proposed to erect a mast at Nork Reservoir, a few yards from these flats, on land owned by Sutton and East Surrey Water PLC. As usual, the residents were not informed; we learnt of the proposal by chance and late in the day. The proposal was rubber-stamped by Reigate and Banstead Borough Council, who ignored more than a hundred letters of protest from residents. The residents then wrote to Sutton and East Surrey Water in their capacities as neighbours and customers;

again, more than a hundred letters were sent. The Residents' Association and the Councillors sitting in their interest came in on the act belatedly, when the work had already been done by others. Eventually Sutton and East Surrey withdrew permission for a mast to be erected on their land. It is possible that Vodafone were losing interest in this mast as a result of local opposition, although they have not admitted this.

In order that you may 'take into account local sensibilities' I urge you to get in touch with Sutton and East Surrey Water and with Vodafone. Why did SESW, after treating local opposition dismissively week after week, eventually give way?

This is highly relevant to your proposed mast at BBM. The BBM site is only a few hundred yards from Nork Reservoir. The people who would be adversely affected are largely the same. I enclose a copy of my letter of 2 June to Mr. R.N. Clifford of Reigate and Banstead.

I have offered BBM to match BT Cellnet's fee, so that they would not lose financially through withdrawing from this arrangement. I made the same offer to Sutton and East Surrey Water.

I am sure you are right that on occasion people have different perspectives on the siting of antennae. Your perspective is apparently to follow due process. My perspective is that the primary and secondary legislation were brought in over ten years or more from the mid-1980s to the mid-1990s. Much has changed over the last fifteen years or more. Health risks are more widely acknowledged or suspected and less readily tolerated than they were. From a rapidly growing collection, I enclose a report from the *Daily Telegraph* of May 24 and a cartoon from the *Daily Mail* of May 25.

In canvassing the district that would be subject to BBM's rays, I found opinion more than ten-to-one against further masts even if this meant forgoing an improvement in the quality of mobile-phone reception. This was true of mobile-phone users and non-users alike.

BT and thus BT Cellnet, like Sutton and East Surrey Water and unlike BBM and apparently Vodafone, have a public image to preserve. I know how important this is to BT from the material I am sent in my capacity as a shareholder. Most of the residents whose interests the BBM mast would damage are BT customers. Many must be BT shareholders.

For what this information may be worth, my family are not Greens, although we recycle everything. My views on environmental matters are pretty much those of the Institute of Economic Affairs, who have published me many times: environmental problems are best resolved by market forces. I have already started writing up the story of these local masts.

My conception of market forces does not include the emission of rays which are or may be dangerous. The hazards have not so far been proved or disproved. Remember the story of asbestos.

I therefore ask you to put this mast on hold while alternatives are considered. The alternatives should include accepting the imperfections, if any, of the present network rather than imposing this unwelcome intrusion on your customers and shareholders. Above all, please do not erect this mast overnight as soon as you have obtained permission from Reigate and Banstead Council.

I look forward to hearing from you.

APPENDIX V

Letter of 9 January 2000 from BB-M to Sir Iain Vallance, Chairman BT

PERSONAL AND URGENT:
DOES BT CELLNET KNOW WHAT IT IS DOING?

BT Cellnet Mast Banstead Station

I have received a letter dated 5 January 2000 (copy attached) from Nadia Bagwell of BT Cellnet's Customer Resolution Team. This was sent by second-class post and reached me at the weekend on Saturday 8 January. She says that the position chosen for the mast is situated in a builder's yard in a low railway cutting. This is wrong. BT Cellnet has no plans to situate a mast in such a position, nor have Reigate and Banstead Borough Council been informed of any such plans for future implementation. The present proposal is to base the mast at road level, which is thirty nine steps above the level of the railway platform and some further feet above the level of the railway. There is no way in which this site could be described as 'in a low railway cutting'. One might as well describe a clifftop site as being 'on the beach'.

Does anyone at BT Cellnet know what is going on? A fundamental and elementary mistake like this implies that the answer is no.

If Nadia Bagwell speaks for BT Cellnet and if after 'the siting of the mast has been carefully considered with all facts borne in mind' 'the chosen position' (is) 'situated in a builder's yard in a low railway cutting', this form of words suggests a way forward. The plain meaning of 'in a low railway cutting' is that the mast would be much lower and less visible than if it were built on the higher land surrounding the cutting. I urge that BT Cellnet resite the mast precisely as Nadia Bagwell indicates. That could provide a solution satisfactory to all concerned. I hope that BT Cellnet and BT are not on course to make a public exhibition of themselves. None of the concerns I put to Nicholas Eldred on 14 June has been addressed.

I was glad to see from Eurofacts 17 December that you have been elected President of the CBI, and I wish you well in presiding over that citadel of political correctness. The initials CBI bring back memories for me. I was Economic Director there from 1968 to 1973, when I left in particular circumstances, as is indicated in the attached note on the author from my forthcoming book about telecommunication masts.

APPENDIX W

The Missing Phone Book

Letter of 7 May 1999 from BB-M to BT Phone Book Manager

I am writing because BT is always one of the most difficult firms to reach by telephone.

I have for many years had an Ambassador 2 + 4. I require two copies, not one, of the Epsom and Leatherhead Area Phone Book. I always require two copies. I nearly always receive one copy. I then have to write to ask for a second copy. When I do so, I ask that two copies, not one, be sent in future. I have lost count of the number of times I have done this. But BT is apparently incapable of providing a second copy without a specific request.

Letter of 11 May from N. J. Dunn, CD Phone Book Advisor, to BB-M

In his letter of 11 May, N. J. Dunn said that BT were unable to access any BT telephone service details from the address I had given them and were therefore, at the moment, unable to send the Phone Book I had requested. If I had service with BT, would I please call them on 0800 243778 and quote my telephone and account numbers and they would be pleased to order a free of charge book for me. If my service was with another communications company, then would I please contact them direct to obtain my copy.

Letter of 20 May from BB-M to N. J. Dunn, CD Phone Book Advisor

Thank you for your letter of 11 May. You explain that you are unable to access any BT telephone service details from the address I have given you. You ask whether my service is with BT or another company.

My service details are given in 'The Phone Book: Epsom and Leatherhead Area' March 1999, page 304, column 2. This is a useful work of reference and I suggest that you obtain a copy.

Alternatively, page 14 of this book mentions another way of resolving your problem. It is called 'Directory Enquiries'. You just dial 192. The service is available 24 hours a day, 7 days a week. It provides telephone numbers from addresses, though not the other way round.

I have lived at this address for thirty-two years. Subject to changes in the area code inflicted on me by British Telecommunications and its predecessors, the number has always been the same. I have always used BT and its predecessors and have never used any other company.

I hope that this information will enable you to 'access BT telephone service details'. I cannot understand why you have found me so elusive.

Letter of 9 November from BB-M to Sir Iain Vallance

I enclose copies of my letter of 7 May to BT Phone Book Manager, Stoke-on-Trent, of N. J. Dunn's reply of 11 May and of my letter of 20 May to N. J. Dunn. As I had had no reply, I sent a copy of my letter to N. J. Dunn by recorded delivery (RT 938 5867 0GB) on 19 July. I have still had no reply.

The inefficiency of your book supply service is breathtaking. Since I can get no sense out of the people in Stoke-on-Trent, I am writing to you in the hope that you will find someone else in your organisation who will provide a second copy of the Epsom and Leatherhead Area Phone Book.

Letter of 15 November from John Rutnam to BB-M

Sir Iain Vallance has asked me to thank you for your letter of 9 November 1999.

I am sorry about the difficulties you have been experiencing. I have arranged for the matter to be looked into and we shall reply to you as soon as possible.

APPENDIX X

Council for the Protection of Rural England: Ten Campaign Tips

1 Campaigners should inquire whether operators have provided details of their district-wide network of masts to local authorities, and discussed it with them.
2 Campaigners should request the local planning authority to inform them of all proposals which do not require a planning application in order to make comments on their impact.
3 Campaigners should persuade the local planning authority to withdraw permitted development rights for telecommunications development where there is a real threat to the local amenity.
4 Campaigners should encourage local planning authorities to include policies on telecommunications development in their development plans which reflect local environmental constraints, and to introduce supplementary planning guidance where appropriate.
5 Campaigners should press local authorities not to consider applications when they have not been provided with all the information they need to make a decision.
6 Campaigners should ask operators to explain why other sites are not acceptable and should put forward their own sites for consideration.

7 Campaigners should ask operators to justify why developers are not placing antennae on existing structures or sharing existing masts in the immediate location.
8 Campaigners should request that the local planning authority employ an expert to deal with contentious applications.
9 Campaigners should request planning conditions which require the local authority to be notified when a mast becomes redundant. These should require the apparatus be removed and the site returned to its original condition.
10 Campaigners should press for planning conditions which reduce the impact of development such as camouflaging the antenna (e.g. as a flagpole on a church) or require landscaping appropriate to the area.